AMERICAN TROUBLEMAKERS

Paul Robeson: A Voice of Struggle

T★AMERICAN★S TROUBLEMAKERS

PAUL ROBESON:
A Voice of Struggle

Burnham Holmes

With an Introduction by James P. Shenton

RSVP

**RAINTREE
STECK-VAUGHN**
P U B L I S H E R S
The Steck-Vaughn Company

Austin, Texas

For Robert Sharma

CONSULTANTS

Michael Kort
Professor of Social Science
Boston University
Boston, Massachusetts

Catherine J. Lenix-Hooker
Executive Director
Krueger-Scott Mansion Cultural
  Center
Newark, New Jersey

MANAGING EDITOR
Richard G. Gallin

PROJECT MANAGER
Julie Klaus

PHOTO EDITOR
Margie Foster

A Gallin House Press Book

Library of Congress Cataloging-in-Publication Data
Holmes, Burnham, 1942-
    Paul Robeson: a voice of struggle / Burnham Holmes; with an introduction by James P. Shenton.
        p.   cm. — (American Troublemakers)
    "A Gallin House Press Book."
    Includes bibliographical references and index.
    ISBN 0-8114-2381-6
    1. Robeson, Paul, 1898-1976 — Juvenile literature.   2. Afro-Americans — Biography — Juvenile literature.   3. Actors —United States — Biography — Juvenile literature.   4. Singers — United States — Biography — Juvenile literature   I.Title.   II. Series.
E185.97.R63H65   1995
782'.0092—dc20
    [B]   94-12665
                                                                                          CIP
                                                                                           AC

Printed and bound in the United States.
1 2 3 4 5 6 7 8 9 0 LB 99 98 97 96 95 94

CONTENTS

Paul Robeson

by James P. Shenton

Biography is the history of the individual lives of men and women. In all lives, there is a sequence that begins with birth, evolves into the development of character in childhood and adolescence, is followed by the emergence of maturity in adulthood, and finally concludes with death. All lives follow this pattern, although with each emerge the differences that make each life unique. These distinctive characteristics are usually determined by the particular area in which a person has been most active. An artist draws his or her specific identity from the area of the arts in which he or she has been most active. So the writer becomes an author; the musician, a performer or composer; the politician, a senator, governor, president, or statesperson. The intellectual discipline to which one is attached identifies the scientist, historian, economist, literary critic, or political scientist, among many. Some aspects of human behavior are identified as heroic, cowardly, corrupt, or just ordinary. The task of the biographer is to explain why a particular life is worth remembering. And if the effort is successful, the reader draws from it insights into a vast range of behavior patterns. In a sense, biography provides lessons from life.

Some lives become important because of the position a person holds. Typical would be that of a U.S. President in which a biographer compares the various incumbents to determine their comparative importance. Without question, Abraham Lincoln was a profoundly significant President, much more so than Warren G. Harding whose administration was swamped by corruption. Others achieve importance because of their role in a particular area. So Emily Dickinson and Carl Sandburg are recognized as important poets and Albert Einstein as a great scientist.

Implicit in the choice of biographical subjects is the idea that each somehow affected history. Their lives explain something about the world in which they lived, even as they affect our lives and that of generations to come. But there is another consideration: Some lives are more interesting than those of others. Within each life is a great story that illuminates human behavior.

Then there are those people who are troublemakers, people whom we cannot ignore. They are the people who both upset and fascinate us. Their singular quality is that they are uniquely different. Troublemakers are irritating, perhaps frightening, frustrating, and disturbing, but never dull. They march to their own drummer and they are original.

To be both black and radical in America has never made for an easy life. Few people demonstrated this more fully than Paul Robeson. The son of a fugitive slave father and a mother from a distinguished black family, he had the advantage—rare for an African American in the early 20th century— of an education at a major U.S. college. As an All-American football player at Rutgers College he revealed an athletic prowess that made him a legend. This skill was complemented by an outstanding academic ability, an eloquence that made him a debater's delight, and an astounding bass-baritone singing voice. Robeson graduated first in his Rutgers class. In spite of his achievements, however, he encountered a great deal of racial discrimination. These experiences gave him a sense of alienation from much of American life.

Soon after graduating from law school, he gave up a career as a lawyer and turned his full attention to acting and singing. Both his speaking and singing voice possessed a power that awed his audiences. To his impressive list of stage performances, including those in *Show Boat* and Shakespeare's *Othello*, he added many films and recordings. By the mid-1930s, Robeson had achieved worldwide fame.

But Robeson could not escape the gnawing realization that segregation continued to burden African Americans. Searching for a better alternative, he favored many causes backed by Communists, including opposition to lynchings, support of the Soviet Union, and help for the anti-Fascist Republican troops in the Spanish Civil War. Many Americans began to view him as a traitor. In the final years of his life, as his health deteriorated, Robeson continued to support radical causes. The denial of human rights, he believed, was a worldwide problem, not just an American one. Painfully, racial discrimination left him a controversial stranger in his own land.

CHAPTER ONE

The Early Years

Paul Robeson grew up in a world that was not far removed from slavery. His father, William Drew Robeson, had lived the life of a slave. In 1860, at the age of 15, Paul's father escaped from a plantation in North Carolina. As William Drew's parents had no last name, Paul's father had taken a variation of Roberson, the slave owner's name. With the assistance of the Underground Railroad, a network of antislavery people who helped Blacks escape from slavery in the South to freedom in the North, William Drew Robeson fled to Pennsylvania.

During the Civil War, Paul Robeson's father worked for the Union Army as a construction worker. When the war ended in 1865, he earned money doing farmwork and studied hard to become a learned man. After finishing school, he began his studies at Lincoln University, an African American college outside of Philadelphia, Pennsylvania. In 1873, he earned a bachelor of arts degree, the degree usually granted after completing four years of college. Three years later, William Drew Robeson completed the requirements for a bachelor of sacred theology for his studies in religious beliefs and practices.

The Reverend William Drew Robeson's first position was as a minister in Wilkes-Barre, Pennsylvania. Two years later, the 33-year-old reverend married 24-year-old Maria Louisa Bustill, a schoolteacher from Philadelphia. Her family had a combination of African, English, and Native American backgrounds and belonged to the Society of Friends, a religious group known as the Quakers. She spoke in the "thee" and "thy" of the Quakers.

Maria Louisa Robeson proved to be a wonderful partner. As Paul later wrote: "She was a companion to him in his studies; she helped compose his sermons; she was his right hand in all his community work."

After Wilkes-Barre, the Robesons went to Princeton, New

Jersey, where Reverend William Drew Robeson became the minister of the Witherspoon Street Presbyterian Church. Princeton turned out to be a good place to live and raise children. There were four older children in the Robeson family—William, 17; Reeve, 12; Benjamin, 6; and Marian, 4—when Paul Leroy Robeson was born on April 9, 1898.

From an early age, Paul was made to feel valued. "[L]ike my father, the people claimed to see something special about me," Paul later observed. "Whatever it was, and no one really said, they felt I was fated for great things to come."

In 1900, after 20 years as the minister, William Drew Robeson was charged by higher church officials with "carelessness" in business matters because the church had not been able to support itself financially. No evidence of wrongdoing was ever offered, and the members of his black congregation stood solidly behind him. Even so, a year later he felt it was best that he resign.

In January of 1904, Maria Louisa Robeson was doing some routine housecleaning. When she and Benjamin moved a small stove in the living room, a burning coal fell and her dress caught on fire. Ben, the only one at home that day, ran to a neighbor's house for help, but by the time he had returned and the fire was put out, Maria Louisa Robeson was badly burned. The doctor arrived and treated her with linseed oil and limewater, as well as opiates to help ease her great pain. Although she was in agony, she maintained a philosophical attitude. "This is the way I am to go," said Maria Louisa Robeson, "and because God intended it I am content." She died a few days later.

"I remember her lying in the coffin, and the funeral, and the relatives who came," Paul later wrote, "but it must be that the pain and shock of her death blotted out all other personal recollections. Others have told me of her remarkable intellect, her strength of character and spirit which contributed so much to my father's development and work."

"There must have been moments when I felt the sorrows of a motherless child," wrote Paul Robeson, who had been only six when his mother died. "[B]ut what I most remember from my youngest days was an abiding sense of comfort and security. I got plenty of mothering, not only from Pop and my brothers and sister when they were home, but from the whole of our close-knit community."

"[T]he people of our small Negro community were, for the most part, a servant class," explained Paul Robeson, "domestics in the homes of the wealthy, serving as cooks, waiters and care-takers at the university, coachmen for the town and laborers at the nearby farms and brickyards."

His father was a heroic figure for the young Paul. "From him we learned, and never doubted it," said Paul, "that the Negro was in every way the equal of the white man." It was sometimes diffi-cult for the Reverend William Drew Robeson—a tall, broad-shouldered, imposing man with a booming voice—to walk down the street because so many people sought out his advice. "The pastor was a sort of bridge between the Have-nots and the Haves," explained Paul, "and he served his flock in many worldly ways—seeking work for the jobless, money for the needy, mercy from the Law."

After losing his position as a minister in Princeton, Paul's father tried his hand at several things: hauling ashes, chauffeur-ing Princeton students, running a grocery store. These were rough times for the father and the two children, Ben and Paul, still living with him. Sometimes the three of them would have only cornbread to eat for all three meals. Through it all, however, the father remained a steadying influence. For no matter how low their fortunes sank, he was "still the dignified Reverend Robeson to the community, and no man carried himself with greater pride."

Paul attended a segregated grade school in Princeton. "I had very little connection with the white people of Princeton," Paul wrote later, "but there were some white children among my play-mates. One of these was a boy, about my age. . . . We could not go to school together, of course, but during the long summer days we were inseparable companions at play."

Eventually, William Drew Robeson started the Downer Street St. Luke A.M.E. Zion Church in Westfield, New Jersey. (A.M.E. stands for African Methodist Episcopal.) Then he moved on to Somerville, New Jersey, to become the minister of the St. Thomas A.M.E. Zion Church.

After moving from Princeton in 1907, Paul attended an integrated school in Westfield. Then he went for one year to that town's all-black Jamison School, graduating at the head of his class. In 1912, Paul went to Somerville High School where he was one of only two African Americans.

"I frequently visited the homes of my schoolmates and always received a friendly welcome. . . ," recalled Paul. "For one thing, I was the respected preacher's son, and then, too, I was popular with the other boys and girls because of my skill at sports and studies, and because I was always ready to share in their larks and fun-making."

Yet, there was an invisible line that Paul felt he could not cross. "Even while demonstrating that he is really an equal (and, strangely, the proof must be *superior* performance!) the Negro must never appear to be challenging white superiority," explained Paul. "Climb up if you can—but don't act 'uppity.'"

Paul's high regard for his father, who was 53 years older, had an enormous influence on him. "[T]here were the winter

Somerville, New Jersey. Paul Robeson spent his childhood in the New Jersey towns of Princeton, Westfield, and Somerville.

evenings at home with Pop: he loved to play checkers and so we two would sit for hours in the parlor, engrossed in our game, not speaking much but wonderfully happy together."

One subject that his father never said anything about was his early years as a slave. "I'm sure that had he ever spoken about this part of his life it would have been utterly impossible for me as a boy to grasp the idea that a noble human being like my father had actually been owned by another man. . . ."

Reverend William Drew Robeson's silence was never uncomfortable for Paul. It was the natural way they acted when they were around each other. "[B]y nature Pop was restrained of speech, often silent at home, and among us Robesons the deepest feelings are largely unexpressed in words. . . ."

One time the son disobeyed his father and ran from him. The father slipped and fell down, knocking out a tooth. Paul felt deep guilt over the experience.

"I have never forgotten the emotions—the sense of horror, shame, ingratitude, selfishness—that overwhelmed me," wrote Paul later. "I adored him, would have given my life for him in a flash—and here I had hurt him, disobeyed him! Never did he have to admonish me again; and this incident became a source of tremendous discipline which has lasted through the years."

Another time his father asked why he had received a B when all his other grades were As. Paul replied that no one ever received 100 percent. Then why did 100 percent exist? his father had wondered aloud. From then on Paul tried hard to get all As.

"But this was not because he made a fetish of perfection," explained Paul. "Rather it was that the concept of *personal integrity*, which was his ruling passion, included inseparably the idea of *maximum human fulfillment*. Success in life was not to be measured in terms of money and personal advancement, but rather the goal must be the richest and highest development of one's own potential."

This quest for excellence in the classroom remained with Paul as the yardstick to use the rest of his life. "I would measure myself only against my own potential and not see myself in competition with anyone else." Like his father before him, Paul would not strive for personal gain and fame, but rather for the development of himself to his highest capacity. His father also set the example for Paul's brothers and sister. Two of Paul's older brothers and his sister went to college. Benjamin and Marian went to Biddle University and Scotia Seminary, respectively, in North Carolina. William went to Lincoln University, the college his father had attended.

The next thing to which Paul applied the discipline and quest for excellence he had gained from his father was athletics. "There were the vacant lots for ball games and the wonderful moments when Bill, vacationing from college where he played on the team, would teach me how to play football," remembered Paul. "He was my first coach, and over and over again on a weed-grown lot he would put me through the paces—how to tackle a man so he stayed tackled, how to run with the ball. "

But it was Ben, a good all-around athlete, who most influenced Paul in sports. "Ben was an outstanding athlete by any standards," said Paul, "and had he attended one of the prominent colleges I'm convinced he would have been chosen All-American. Certainly he ranked in ability with many of the famous stars I later encountered in college games and professional football." Ben was also a baseball player of major-league caliber, but in those days, African Americans were not allowed to play in the big leagues.

But Ben not only played sports with Paul, he also took his 14-year-old brother to the summer resort town of Narragansett Pier, Rhode Island, to work as a busboy, removing dirty dishes and resetting tables, and as a waiter. It was the first time that Paul had ever been outside New Jersey. Paul kept this job throughout his teens as a way to make money during the summer.

It was in schoolwork that Paul's brother William really made his mark on Paul. Nicknamed "W.D." and "Schoolboy," William was an excellent student (he was to become a medical doctor) who helped Paul learn how to study. This was extremely important for Paul because he had classes in Greek, Latin, history, literature, and philosophy. In particular, William taught Paul not to be satisfied simply with the correct answer but to look for how one fact is related to another.

Paul's course of study can be viewed in light of the two leading black educators who had greatly influenced the education of African Americans. One was Booker T. Washington of Tuskegee Institute. He had encouraged African Americans to be practical and go to trade schools so that they would be able to get steady jobs that called for skills, jobs in trades such as those practiced by electricians and plumbers and jobs in factories and agriculture. According to Washington, instead of demanding an end to racial segregation and discrimination, African Americans should become economically powerful. In that way they would gain respect and eventually equal civil rights.

The other educator was W. E. B. Du Bois, who believed that African Americans were not going to end racial segregation and discrimination simply by gaining economic security. African Americans would have to protest against discrimination. They should demand equal rights. Moreover, the brightest African Americans should be encouraged to go to college and become professionals such as doctors, teachers, and lawyers. Du Bois, who had helped found the National Association for the Advancement of Colored People, encouraged African Americans to study the classics, in order to get a well-rounded liberal arts education. "Education must not simply teach work," believed Du Bois, "it must teach life."

Another of Paul's brothers who had an influence on him, but for an entirely different reason, was Reeve. Reeve was a coachman with a fiery spirit who was always getting into one scrape after another, especially with Princeton students who displayed prejudice toward him. "Yet I admired this rough older brother and I learned from him a quick militancy against racial insults and abuse." "Don't ever take low" is the lesson that Reeve instilled in Paul. "Stand up to them and hit back harder than they hit you!" Judging by Paul Robeson's later life, it would seem that Paul was as influenced by Reeve Robeson as he was by his other brothers.

Paul also had his sister as an example of the quest for excellence in the classroom. Like her mother before her, Marian Robeson went on to become a schoolteacher. "If it turned out that it was to be Ben who followed my father's calling as a minister," said Paul, "it was Marian who continued the teaching traditions of my mother's family." Also similar to her mother, Marian did not feel any limitations because she was a woman, and a black woman at that.

The youngest Robeson excelled in many sports in high school. Not only was Paul a fullback in football, where he attracted attention from around the state, but he was also a shortstop and catcher in baseball, a center on the basketball team, and a runner in track. Paul even excelled in tennis.

Paul displayed other talents as well. He achieved success as a debater and public speaker, winning third prize in a New Jersey oratorical contest. The theme of his speech was what American abolitionist and reformer Wendell Phillips had quoted from Toussaint-Louverture, the Haitian general and leader of Haiti's independence movement against France: "My children, France comes to make us slaves. God gave us liberty; France has no right to take it away."

The biggest influence in Paul's use of language had been his father. At home he had been influenced by the precise diction of Reverend William Drew Robeson. Ever since he was a small boy, Paul had been listening to the melodious eloquence of his

Robeson and the Somerville High School football team in 1913.
He also was a runner and played baseball, basketball, and tennis.

father's sermons. "I heard . . . songs in the very sermons of my father," said Paul, "for in the Negro's speech there is much of the phrasing and rhythms of folk-song."

The youngest Robeson's rich bass voice was beginning to attract attention, too. One of the first times was right at home with his brothers. Although William, Benjamin, and Paul had just been fooling around singing a few songs, William realized that his brother possessed talent. "Wait a minute, hit that note again, Paul," he had said. Paul sang it over again. "Paul," William said, "you can sing."

Ben later said that Paul's singing career "started that July afternoon [in 1910], with Bill, Paul and myself. Without that happening, I doubt if he would ever have been near any singing group."

On Sunday, Paul began singing in the choir at his father's church. "[T]here was a warmth of song," remembered Paul. "Songs of love and longing, songs of trials and triumphs, deep-flowing rivers and rollicking brooks, hymn-song and ragtime ballad, gospels and blues, and the healing comfort to be found in the illimitable sorrow of the spirituals."

Later Paul joined the glee club at Somerville High School. The director of the glee club and music teacher, Elizabeth Vosseller, was the first to help him develop his natural talents as a singer.

Another teacher, Anna Miller, coached Paul in the title role in a high-school parody of William Shakespeare's *Othello.* "Nervous and scared, I struggled through the lines on that solemn occasion. . . ," Paul later remembered, "and no one in the world could have convinced me then that I should ever try acting again." Ironically, it would be his portrayal of Othello several years later that would play such an important role in his life.

Two other teachers were also instrumental in helping form the young Robeson's attitudes. Miss Vandeveer, the Latin teacher, taught racial equality by setting an example. Miss Bagg, the chemistry and physics teacher, made Robeson feel accepted in this almost all-white high school.

There was one person at Somerville High School who was totally unhelpful, however, and that was the principal. Dr. Ackerman did not like the success that Paul was achieving in scholarship, athletics,

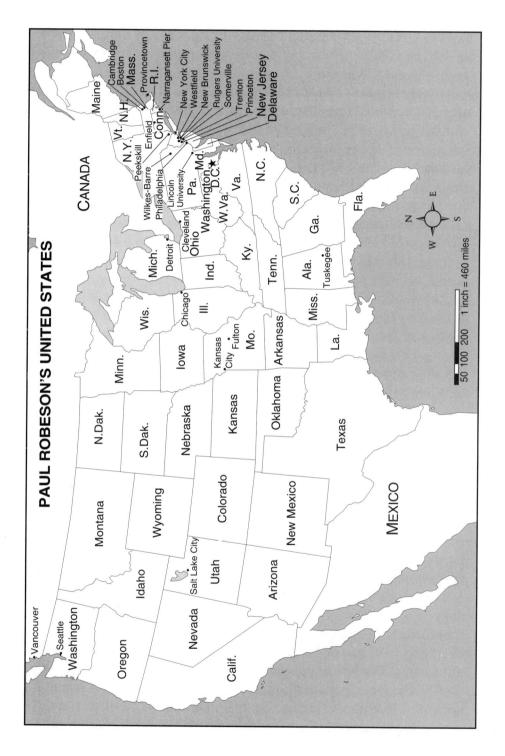

PAUL ROBESON'S UNITED STATES

and extracurricular activities. Consequently, at every opportunity he put obstacles in Paul's way. "I don't care what *you* do to me," Paul lashed out in conversation with his father. "[B]ut if that hateful old principal ever lays a hand on me, I swear I'll try my best to break his neck!"

The easiest path for Paul would have been to follow in his father's and brother's footsteps and go to Lincoln University. During his senior year in high school, however, Paul learned about an exam for a four-year scholarship to Rutgers College. Most of the other competing students had taken a three-hour test earlier that year covering the first three years and now were taking another three-hour test that dealt only with their senior year. Paul, on the other hand, was taking only one three-hour test that ranged over all four high school years. In addition, many of the other students had been preparing for this test for a long time, whereas Paul had only recently heard about it. Nevertheless, Paul was one of the winners.

Years later, Paul Robeson would see his winning this scholarship as a turning point in his life. *"Deep in my heart from that day on,"* wrote Paul, *"was a conviction which none of the Ackermans of America would ever be able to shake.* Equality might be denied, but I *knew* I was not inferior."

But there remained other uncertainties. One was what should Paul do with his life.

"When I was seventeen and in my final semester at high school, I still had no vocation in mind. Singer? No, that was just for fun. Dramatics? Not I! There was the lingering thought, never too definite, of studying for the ministry; and though my father would have liked that choice, he never pressed it upon me. Perhaps in college I'd come to a decision about a career."

CHAPTER TWO

"Robeson of Rutgers"

Established in 1766, Rutgers College, "on the banks of the old Raritan" in New Brunswick, New Jersey, was one of the nation's oldest colleges. In 1915, 17-year-old Paul Robeson entered Rutgers, becoming the only African American among the 500 students on campus and only the third Black ever to attend the college (now Rutgers University). Paul also became the first African American ever to try out for the Rutgers football team. Even at that time, Rutgers had a long history of football. As a matter of fact, Rutgers had played in the first collegiate football game ever—a game with Princeton University in 1869. So the prejudice against having any Blacks on the football team was deep seated.

At Paul Robeson's very first scrimmage, or practice, he was double-teamed—blocked with two players at one time—and gang-tackled—brought down with several tacklers—again and again. The flimsy leather helmet and the skimpy padding that in those days players wore underneath their jerseys and knickers did not provide much protection.

Afterward, Paul hobbled back to his room in a private home (he was not allowed to live in a college dormitory), suffering from bruises, cuts, and a broken nose. He was so battered that he had to spend the following week in bed. Paul may never have returned except for one thing. His father had instilled in his youngest son the belief that he was a representative of his people not only in the classroom but also on the athletic field. "[A]nd as their representative, I had to show that I could take whatever they handed out. . . . This was part of our struggle."

Fortunately, Paul's brother William visited him that week. "Kid, I know what it is," William told him. "I went through it at Pennsylvania. If you want to quit school go ahead, but I wouldn't like to think, and our father wouldn't like to think, that our family had a quitter."

Paul Robeson on the Rutgers College football team. He became a two-time All-American football player.

After recovering from his injuries, Paul returned for another practice session. Once again, his teammates began to gang up on him. The last straw was when one of the players intentionally stomped on Robeson's hand as he was lying on the ground. On the next play, Robeson tackled the ball carrier and lifted him off the ground. "It wasn't a thought, it was just a feeling, to kill," said Paul. "I got Kelly in my two hands and I got him up over my head. . . . I was going to smash him so hard to the ground that I'd break him right in two."

George Foster Sanford, the Rutgers coach, stepped in, blowing his whistle furiously. "Robeson, you're on the varsity," the coach yelled. Later on, Coach Sanford held a short meeting. He informed his players not only that Paul Robeson had made the team, but also that the next player who attempted to hurt him would be kicked off the squad.

That year Robeson worked hard on blocking, tackling, and pass catching. Before the season was over, he was a member of the starting team. Although his own teammates no longer tried to rough him up, other teams did. Robeson, however, stood his ground.

After one particularly rough game, Earl "Greasy" Neale, the coach of the West Virginia team (and later the coach of the Philadelphia Eagles) exclaimed, "Why that colored boy's legs were so gashed and bruised that his skin peeled off when he removed his stockings."

Following a home game on another afternoon, Paul discussed his play with his favorite fan, who had been sitting in the stands, Reverend William Drew Robeson.

"Gee, Dad, if I'd just made that touchdown the last few minutes of the game, I'd have played a perfect game today."

"But, son, you made three touchdowns, and nobody else made any."

"I know, Dad, but I *could* have and *should* have made a fourth."

Paul usually brought this same intensity and pursuit of excellence to the classroom. From time to time, however, his father needed to issue a reminder: "You mustn't forget your studies for your games, son; you went to school for study, not to play. I'm

22

glad that you can play, but you mustn't forget the real reason why you went to college."

After his first two years at Rutgers, Paul still didn't know what career he wanted to enter. "A minister like my father? A teacher like my mother? Maybe. But whatever the vocation might be, I must grow up to be a 'credit to the race.'"

In 1917, his junior year, Robeson started to attract wide attention for his football playing. Stories about the exploits of Paul Robeson on the football field at first appeared only in the *Targum*, the student newspaper at Rutgers College. Eventually, however, these accounts about "Robeson of Rutgers" found their way into the major New York newspapers.

Charles A. Taylor, for example, wrote an article in the *New York Tribune*, on October 28, 1917, about a game that Rutgers won 28 to 0:

> A dark cloud upset the hopes of the Fordham eleven yesterday afternoon. Its name was Robeson. . . .
>
> Robeson, the giant Negro, appeared in the line-up as left end, but he did not confine himself to this particular post. He played in turn practically every position in the Rutgers team before the game was ended.
>
> With his team on the offensive, Robeson was wont to leap high in the air to grab forward passes wherever he saw that a man they were intended for was in another sector of the battle field. On the defence he was kept busy on the few occasions when Fordham appeared likely to make a score. . . .
>
> It would be wrong to say that Robeson is the entire Rutgers team. The aggregation is too well balanced for that, but it was this dark cloud that cut off all the sunshine for the Fordham rooters yesterday.

On November 25, 1917, Louis Lee Arms reported another game in the *New York Sunday Tribune*, a game between Rutgers College and the Newport Naval Reserves:

A tall, tapering Negro in a faded crimson sweater, moleskins, and a pair of maroon socks ranged hither and yon on a wind-whipped Flatbush field yesterday afternoon. . . .

It was Robeson, a veritable Othello of battle, who led the dashing little Rutgers eleven to a 14-0 victory over the widely heralded Newport Naval Reserves. . . .

As a thorn in her [the Newport Naval Reserve team's] flesh the tall, tapering Robeson, commanding Rutgers' secondary, dived under and spilled her wide, oblique angled runs, turned back her line plunges, and carried the burden of the defence so splendidly that in forty-four minutes these ex-All-American backs, who are fixed luminaries in the mythology of the gridiron, made precisely two first downs. . . .

Among the original tactical manoeuvres in Rutgers' attack is the calling in of Robeson to open holes for the back field. He is shifted by signal from left end to whatever spot along the line had been pre-selected. Thus considerable of Rutgers' line drives were put upon the basis of Robeson's superiority over Black, Schlacter, Callahan, or whomever he faced.

Robeson was not only fast, but at six feet three inches and 217 pounds, he was big for his day. A sure-handed pass receiver, he was so good a blocker that he was switched from end to tackle in short yardage situations. And on defense (in those days, players often played on both offense and defense), Robeson was one of the best middle linebackers in the country. As George Daly wrote in the *New York World* on November 28, 1917:

ROBESON TAKES A PLACE
WITH ELECT OF FOOTBALL
*All Around Ability of Rutgers' End Puts Him with
Greatest and Best of the Game*
Paul Robeson, the big Negro end of the Rutgers

eleven, is a football genius. . . .

[H]ere are some of the duties imposed on this super-man of the game:

Opening up holes for his backs on line plays; providing remarkable interference for his backs on end runs; going down the field under punts; taking forward passes, in which, by the way, he handles the pigskin with almost the same sureness as a baseball; supporting the centre of the line on defence, or, as some have it, playing "defensive quarterback"; plugging up holes from one end of the line to the other; tackling here, there, and everywhere; kicking off and diagnosing.

And the greatest perhaps of his accomplishments is accurate diagnosing. His ability to size up plays and quickly get to the point of danger is almost uncanny. He is so rarely at fault that he is at the centre of practically every play, and therein lies his greatest value, and therein is the truest measure of his all-around ability.

In 1917 and again in 1918, Robeson was selected to be on the All-American team. Walter Camp, the person who made the selections, stated that "there never was a more serviceable end, both on attack and defense, than Robeson, the 200-pound giant of Rutgers."

This terrific athlete won 15 varsity letters in four varsity sports. In addition to starring in football, Robeson played center on the basketball team, and in track and field he hurled the discuss, the javelin, and the shot put. He was also the catcher on the baseball team. In his final senior-year baseball game, Robeson led Rutgers to a 5 to 1 win over Princeton. It was the first time in 50 years—since the country's first football game in 1869—that Rutgers had beaten Princeton in any sport.

However, it wasn't only on the athletic fields that Robeson achieved prominence. "Robey" (his campus nickname) was a member of the student council. He was a champion debater as well as the captain of the Rutgers debating society. He won the

Paul Robeson on the Rutgers debating team. He also earned Phi Beta Kappa honors and graduated as valedictorian of his class.

rhetorical contest in extemporaneous speaking every year. And during his junior year, Robeson was inducted into Phi Beta Kappa, the national honor society for college students who distinguish themselves in the classroom.

But in the midst of all his successes, Paul Robeson lost the person closest and dearest to him. On May 17, 1918, his father, the Reverend William Drew Robeson, died at the age of 73. "The death of Rev. W. D. Robeson takes from this community one who has done a quiet but successful work among his own people for the past eight years," began an editorial in the Somerville newspaper. "Mr. Robeson was a man of strong character. . . . He had the temperament which has produced so many orators in the South and he held his people together in the church here with a fine discernment of their needs. He has left his impress on the colored race throughout the State and he will be greatly missed here."

There was another person, however, who became important to Paul during his last two years at Rutgers. Geraldine Maimie Neale, who was studying to be a kindergarten teacher at nearby

Teachers Normal School in Trenton, had with the help of Paul successfully changed her college's regulations to allow the integration of the dormitories. Paul was in love with Gerry and repeatedly asked her to be his wife. Although attracted to Paul Robeson, Gerry Neale nevertheless refused because she saw him as having a future that would make it difficult for a marriage to survive.

Paul's senior thesis was titled "The Fourteenth Amendment: 'The Sleeping Giant of the American Constitution.'" This amendment can be used to insure that all U.S. citizens are entitled to their civil rights. Paul argued that because this amendment was being ignored in some parts of the country, Blacks were being denied their rights to vote and to go to the schools of their choice.

During Paul's last year at Rutgers he was chosen to be a member of Cap and Skull, the senior honor society that each year honored four students who had achieved distinction in scholarship, athletics, and character.

Paul Robeson also became the valedictorian of his graduating class. The valedictorian is the student who graduates with the highest grades in the class. One of the honors that the valedictorian receives is that of delivering a speech at the commencement ceremony during which diplomas are conferred on the graduates. The title of Robeson's speech was "The New Idealism."

"We of this less favored race realize that our future lies chiefly in our own hands," Paul Robeson said to the students and parents before him at the commencement. "On ourselves alone will depend the preservation of our liberties and the transmission of them in their integrity to those who will come after us." But at the same time he appealed to "you of the favored race [to] catch a new vision" in order to bring about "equal opportunities for all."

"And we are struggling on," continued the valedictorian of the Rutgers College class of 1919, "attempting to show that knowledge can be obtained under difficulties; that poverty may give place to affluence; that obscurity is not an absolute bar to distinction . . . that neither the old-time slavery, nor continued prejudice need extinguish self-respect, crush manly ambition or paralyze effort; that no power outside of himself can prevent man

27

from sustaining an honorable character and a useful relation to his day and generation."

Paul Robeson had finished another important chapter in his development. His life lay before him full of promise as well as uncertainties, hopes, and dreams. Robeson's first important stop would be Harlem, the northern section of Manhattan Island in New York City.

CHAPTER THREE

Robeson's Career Takes Wing

In the fall of 1919, Paul Robeson began studying law at Columbia University in New York City. To make money for his law school tuition, Robeson not only helped out Coach George Foster Sanford back at Rutgers, but he also played football on the weekends for professional teams. Over the next two years Robeson led the Akron Pros to 18 straight wins. And in 1922, Robeson scored both touchdowns in a 13 to 0 Milwaukee Badgers victory over the Oorang Indians.

Paul Robeson attended Columbia University's School of Law.

The star of the Indians was none other than Native American Jim Thorpe, one of the world's greatest athletes. Thorpe had won the pentathlon and decathlon at the 1912 Olympic Games; from 1913 to 1919, he had played major-league baseball; in 1920, he had begun his professional football career.

But the pro games were even rougher than the college games had been. One fall afternoon in 1920, Robeson hurt his thigh and had to have an operation. It was while he was recovering at Columbia

29

Presbyterian Medical Center in New York City that he met Eslanda Cardozo Goode.

"Essie," as she was known, had like Paul won a four-year college scholarship. She came from a very prominent family. After the Civil War, Eslanda Cardozo Goode's grandfather had been South Carolina's first African American secretary of the treasury. She had spent her childhood in Washington, D.C., and then in New York City. After attending the University of Illinois, Essie Goode had completed her studies at Columbia and had taken a job as an analytical chemist at Columbia Presbyterian. Goode was the first African American to be employed in a staff position in the Surgery and Pathology Department.

In spite of their differences in background and personality, Paul Robeson and Essie Goode were very much attracted to each other. As she once observed: "His education was literary, classical, mine was entirely scientific; his temperament was artistic, mine strictly practical; he is vague, I am definite. . . ."

But opposites sometimes do attract, and their friendship blossomed. Also, Essie Goode was always one for a challenge. "I thought since all the girls were making such a fuss over him, I would try being casual and indifferent," she recalled. "It was just one of those things—it worked." It certainly did. On August 17, 1921, Paul Robeson and Eslanda Cardozo Goode were married.

The year before, Robeson had been influenced by some friends to play the lead in *Simon the Cyrenian*, a play written by Ridgely Torrence about a black African who wanted to save Jesus from the Romans. Jesus, however, talked him out of it. Simon, instead, helped Jesus carry the cross. Several theater people who had seen the play at the Harlem YWCA suggested to those casting another play, *Taboo*, that Robeson play the lead. Paul tried out and got the part. He would be playing opposite Margaret Wycherly, a popular English actress of the day. This was his first professional acting role. Robeson continued with his law studies while preparing for the play.

Taboo was a melodrama written by Mary Hoyt Wiborg about a plantation in Louisiana in desperate need of rain. Although this play at the Sam Harris Theater did not receive particularly good reviews, Robeson did. Most impressed of all was Alexander

Columbia University in New York City. While Paul Robeson attended law school, he met Eslanda Cardozo Goode in 1920.

Woollcott, the drama critic of the *New York Times*. Woollcott was also one of the leaders of the Algonquin Round Table. This was the brilliant group of people in the arts who regularly gathered together for lunch at the Algonquin Hotel. "Perhaps I am only being wise after the event," Woollcott later wrote, "but I think I felt at the time that I had just crossed the path of someone touched by destiny. He was a young man on his way. He did not know where he was going, but I never in my life saw anyone so quietly sure, by some inner knowledge, that he was going somewhere."

Two months later, after *Taboo* had closed its New York run, Robeson was walking down the street and met Harold Browning. Browning was one of the members of The Harmony Kings, who at that time were appearing in the all-black musical revue *Shuffle Along*, written by Noble Sissle and composed by Eubie Blake. Having once heard Robeson sing at a party, Browning asked if he would take over the bass part in their singing quartet. After only one day of rehearsal, Robeson was singing on Broadway—the fabled street and area of New York City where many of the theaters are located. Robeson was stopping the show when he stepped forward to sing the Stephen Foster song "Old Black Joe."

Essie was actively encouraging her husband to explore the possibilities of a career in the theater. So when Paul was asked if he would travel to England in July 1922 for the London production of *Voodoo*, the new title of *Taboo*, he was quick to accept. The play would star Mrs. Patrick Campbell, one of England's most famous actresses.

"At this time I was an aspiring lawyer," said Robeson, "believing that to succeed would help raise my people, the Black people of the world. Theater and concerts were furthest from my mind; this trip was just a lark. Instead of waiting on tables in hotels to earn money, I was being paid twenty pounds [about $80] or so a week for expenses to walk on a stage, say a few lines, sing a song or two. Just too good for words."

Although the play closed in out-of-town performances before ever reaching London, Paul Robeson did meet Lawrence Brown, an accomplished accompanist who played the piano for singers and who was also working on a collection of Negro spirituals. Brown studied and listened to these traditional religious songs and transcribed them, that is, wrote down the words and music.

When Robeson returned to New York, there was little work for him in the theater. So once again, he threw himself into the study of law. In February 1923, Robeson graduated from the Columbia University School of Law.

In June, he went to work for the law office of Stotesbury and Miner. Louis William Stotesbury, who had also graduated from Rutgers College, liked to help former Rutgers athletes begin their law careers. Robeson became the only African American employed at the law firm and worked on one of the firm's most important cases. It was the contested will of George Jay Gould, a prominent railroad owner and one of the richest stock speculators on Wall Street. The brief (an outline of the major points and evidence) that Robeson developed became one of the blueprints for the case when it finally went to court.

After such a promising beginning, things took a turn for the worse when one of the law firm's secretaries refused to work for Robeson because he was black. An understandably upset Robeson talked over the problem with Stotesbury. Both men realized that if an employee of the firm would not cooperate with him, someday it might be even more difficult with a rich white client whose business the firm desired. As a solution, Stotesbury suggested that Robeson could run a branch law office they would open in Harlem. But Robeson was beginning to feel that the field of law was not for him. His future seemed too limited. He decided to wait for something bigger and better to come along. Robeson wanted to see what else life might have to offer.

That fall, Kenneth Macgowan, the director of the Provincetown Players, contacted Robeson. Macgowan, who along with Eugene O'Neill, had seen Robeson in *Taboo,* was casting for O'Neill's play *All God's Chillun Got Wings.* O'Neill had already won the Pulitzer Prize for his *Beyond the Horizon*—and would go on to win the Nobel Prize for Literature in 1936.

Paul Robeson went down to the Provincetown Playhouse on MacDougal Street in Greenwich Village, a section of New York City where many authors, students, and artists lived and worked. The Provincetown Playhouse had gotten its start and name in Provincetown, Massachusetts, on Cape Cod. It was a group that brought together the talents of playwright Eugene O'Neill, poets Edward Estlin Cummings (better known as e. e. cummings) and Edna St. Vincent Millay, novelists Theodore Dreiser and Edna Ferber, and critic Edmund Wilson—people who wanted to establish a theater of realism.

The Provincetown Players immediately took a liking to Robeson. O'Neill found him to be "a young fellow with considerable experience, wonderful presence and voice, full of ambition and a . . . fine man personally with real brains—not a 'ham.'" Robeson auditioned and won the lead role.

Robeson took a liking to them as well. The Provincetown Players "form one of the most intelligent, sincere, and non-commercial of the artistic groups in America," remarked Essie Robeson. "It is small wonder that when Paul Robeson came to work with them he fell under their spell. . . ."

To top it off, acting represented an income. "I needed money," admitted Robeson. "The [$]75 a week which they offered me was a good salary in those days and I accepted." In fact, at that time public school teachers, for example, earned on average of about $1,200 a year.

All God's Chillun Got Wings was to open in late spring of 1924. Before then, the script was published in the magazine *American Mercury.* The public was able to read it first before seeing it.

The play opens with Ella Downey, a young white girl, and Jim Harris, a young African American boy, playing in the street. The time shifts to nine years later. Because her friends are prejudiced, Ella (later played by Mary Blair) now has little to do with Jim (the role taken by Paul Robeson). When Mickey, her boxer-boyfriend, leaves her with a child, Ella is caught in a web of despair. Even after the child dies, Ella faces a bleak future as a prostitute. But Jim still loves her and asks her to marry him. She consents and they leave for France to escape the racism of America. Two years later, however, they are back in the United States. The play ends with Ella, who has now gone insane, sitting at Jim's feet and kissing his hand.

A storm of protest broke out in the press. This can best be understood against the backdrop of life in 1924: After World War I, race riots had erupted in many cities throughout the United States. Bigotry was on the rise, with a revived racist Ku Klux Klan claiming a membership of 8 million Americans in 1924. Racial segregation in schools, restaurants, hotels, and housing was enforced by laws in most of the South and by tradition in much of the North. More than half of the states in the United States did not allow Blacks and Whites to marry. Some newspaper articles predicted that the play would result in riots. To defuse the situation, the Provincetown Players decided to open with another O'Neill play, *The Emperor Jones.* Then they would put on *All God's Chillun Got Wings.*

Paul Robeson would also have the lead in *The Emperor Jones.* In the original 1920 production, Charles Gilpin had played the lead and had won acclaim. In fact, the National Association for the Advancement of Colored People (NAACP) had awarded Gilpin its prestigious Spingarn Medal for his performance.

Although Gilpin wanted to play the part of Brutus Jones again, Eugene O'Neill had found him too difficult to work with. O'Neill and the director of the play, James Light, preferred Robeson in this role.

So, instead of just one play, Robeson now had to study the lines of two leading roles and rehearse two plays. Paul learned his lines for Brutus Jones by making a game of it. He and Essie went about their day-to-day life together by incorporating speeches from the play.

Rehearsals at the Provincetown Playhouse were another matter altogether. One day James Light, the director of the play, said to Robeson: "[Y]ou look as though you're afraid to move."

"I am," replied Robeson. "I'm so big I feel if I take a few steps I'll be off this tiny stage."

"Then just take two steps, but make them fit you," coached the director. "You must have complete freedom and control over your body and your voice, if you are to control your audience."

The Emperor Jones opened on May 6, 1924. The play takes place on a tropical island and has eight scenes. The action follows Brutus Jones, a onetime railway porter who has become the emperor of the island; however, he has been overthrown and is now fleeing the palace for what he hopes will be the safety of the jungle. As the islanders close in on him, Jones talks and talks. He is visibly cracking under the strain. During one scene Paul was supposed to whistle, but when the director heard him sing, a Negro spiritual was added instead.

The drama critic of the *New York Telegram and Evening Mail* wrote of the audience's reaction to Robeson's performance on opening night:

> [They] rose to their feet and applauded. When the ache in their arms stopped their hands, they used their voices, shouted meaningless words, gave hoarse throaty cries. . . . [T]he ovation was for Robeson, for his emotional strength, for his superb acting.

The opening of *All God's Chillun Got Wings* was set for May 15.

35

The mayor of New York City, Michael Hylan, had refused to allow children to be used in the first scene. Although the city had to approve all use of child actors, permission for such child performances was routinely granted. To deal with this crisis, the director came out and read the scene before the play began.

"When I went on to the stage," Robeson remarked afterward, "I half expected to hear shots from the stalls." But there were none. As a matter of fact, the critics saw the play as rather weak. The reaction to Robeson, however, was far different.

Paul Robeson stars with Mary Blair in the 1924 production of Eugene O'Neill's play *All God's Chillun Got Wings.*

Lawrence Stallings in the June 21, 1924, issue of the *American Mercury* wrote:

> And who has a better voice for tragedy than this actor, whose tone and resonance suggest nothing so much as the dusky, poetic quality of a Negro spiritual, certainly the most tragic utterances in American life? . . .
>
> Solely interested in Robeson's great qualities and in the stage, one wonders if he will play Othello some day. . . . After seeing Robeson's performance in *All God's Chillun*, one can imagine that Shakespeare must have thought of Robeson.

One of the country's most important critics, George Jean Nathan, wrote in the *American Mercury* of July 1924:

> The performance, in the one play as in the other—and no two plays were ever more dissimilar—is hot in its blind illumination. . . . The effect is of a soul bombarded by thunder and torn by lightning. . . . Robeson, with relatively little experience and with no training to speak of, is one of the most thoroughly eloquent, impressive, and convincing actors that I have looked at and listened to in almost twenty years of professional theatre-going."

Paul Robeson appeared in both plays until July. Then he was in *Chillun* until it closed in October. It was long enough for him to realize that he wanted his future to be in the theater. As Essie Robeson wrote: "Apparently he could act—everyone said he could—Jimmy [James Light], Gene [Eugene O'Neill], critics, audiences, and last, but most important, his precious instinct which always guided him, told him that he was on the right road." Unfortunately, no other plays were immediately offered to him.

For the time being, Robeson posed for a sculptor, Antonio Salemmé. He was enjoying being in the company of Salemmé and other intellectuals, both white and African American.

It was a heady period to be living in New York. The 1920s witnessed the height of the literary and artistic movement known as the Harlem Renaissance. This was a period of awakening for all the arts in the African American community of Harlem. In literature, there were among others the poets and novelists Countee Cullen and Langston Hughes and the writers James Weldon Johnson and Claude McKay. In music, there were such performers as trumpeter Louis Armstrong, composer-pianist Edward Kennedy "Duke" Ellington, and jazz singer Elizabeth "Bessie" Smith.

More and more, Essie Robeson filled in as her husband's agent, or business representative, even finding the first movie role for him. It was a silent film called *Body and Soul* by African American filmmaker Oscar Micheaux. In the 1920s, Micheaux was the most prolific filmmaker of stories about black people. The story revolved around a minister, who was bad, and his brother, who was good. Both parts were played by Robeson.

Robeson was also singing more frequently, although primarily at dinner parties and private gatherings. Nevertheless, he was also beginning to give public recitals and concerts. Despite Robeson's growing fame, Paul and Essie Robeson still met with racial discrimination when making hotel, train, and even theater reservations.

In the spring of 1925, Paul Robeson encountered Lawrence "Larry" Brown on the streets of Harlem. These two began getting together to practice the spirituals that Brown had transcribed. One night they performed at a dinner party at writer Carl Van Vechten's. The guests were so enthusiastic that a concert was scheduled for the Greenwich Village Theatre, also owned by the Provincetown Theater.

The day before the concert, journalist Heywood Broun of the *New York World* recommended it to all the readers of his newspaper column, "It Seems to Me." Broun finished with these words: "If Lawrence Brown's arrangement of 'Joshua Fit de Battle ob Jericho' does not turn out to be one of the most exciting experiences in your life, write and tell me about it."

The next evening, April 19, 1925, more people arrived than there were seats. They stood in the wings of the theater and even in the street. Paul Robeson and Larry Brown walked out onto a bare stage. Accompanied by Brown, Robeson sang Negro spirituals. The audience listened to one spiritual after another, songs such as "Go Down, Moses," "Swing Low, Sweet Chariot," "Joshua Fit the Battle of Jericho," "By an' By," "Scandalize My Name," "Steal Away," and "Water Boy." After the final note of each song, expertly arranged by Larry Brown, the audience broke into thunderous applause.

After many encores, Brown and Robeson were exhausted. They "could only bow and smile their appreciation to the still applauding audience," observed Essie Robeson. "It was a memorable evening."

The reviews for this concert were nothing short of ecstatic. According to the *New York Times* critic:

> His Negro Spirituals have the ring of the revivalist, they hold in them a world of religious experience; it is their cry from the depths, this universal humanism, that touches the heart. . . . Mr. Robeson's gift is to make them tell [have a marked effect] in every line, and that not by any outward stress, but by an overwhelming inward conviction. Sung by one man, they voiced the sorrow and hopes of a people.

Heywood Broun wrote about this historic evening:

> All those who listened last night to the first concert in this country made entirely of Negro music . . . may have been present at a turning point, one of those thin points of time in which a star is born and not yet visible—the first appearance of this folk wealth to be made without deference or apology. Paul Robeson's voice is difficult to describe. It is a voice in which deep bells ring.

CHAPTER FOUR

Two Performances of a Lifetime

In August 1925, Essie and Paul Robeson sailed to England to prepare for the London production of *The Emperor Jones* opening in October. It was in London that the Robesons enjoyed their newfound freedom. They were able to come and go as they pleased, to eat in whatever restaurant caught their fancy.

Essie Robeson explained why her husband loved England so and felt more comfortable there than he did in the United States. "The calm, homely beauty and comfort of London, the more leisurely and deliberate pace of life as compared to the general rush and hustle of New York," she wrote, "the whole-hearted friendliness and unreserved appreciation of audiences and of the public at large appealed to him, and inspired him to his best work."

Although the London critics and audiences praised Robeson, they were less enthusiastic about the production of *The Emperor Jones*. It seemed that there was a nonstop beating of drums that grated on their nerves. After only five weeks, the play had run its course and closed.

The Robesons, however, were thoroughly enjoying the people they were meeting. One person in particular was the anarchist who had once been a strong supporter of the Russian Revolution of 1917, Emma Goldman. In recent years, though, she had become disillusioned by the number of Russians imprisoned and killed by the Communists. Robeson and Goldman spent many hours talking together. It was to mark the beginning of Robeson's growing interest in politics.

Essie and Paul Robeson also traveled to the European continent so that he could appear in concerts. In Paris, the Robesons met Ernest Hemingway, James Joyce, and Gertrude Stein—three of the major writers of the 20th century. Gertrude Stein even included Robeson in her book, *The Autobiography of Alice B.*

Toklas, writing that: "He knew american [Stein sometimes did not use capital letters] values and american life as only one in it but not of it could know them."

By the beginning of 1926, the Robesons were back in the United States. It was a busy time for Paul Robeson and his accompanist Larry Brown. First, there were major concert tours. Two concerts in particular stood out. One was in Chicago. Having received almost no publicity, the concert attracted a very small audience. Even so, Robeson and Brown put on a memorable performance.

Herman Devries of the *Chicago Evening American* wrote: "His diction is so clear and intelligible that one needs no programme notes. . . ." Edward Moore of the *Chicago Daily Tribune* said that his voice "never rumbled, never seemed to grow loud, it was always velvety, but it filled the whole expanse of Orchestra Hall. . . ."

Boston, on the other hand, was a completely different story. Robeson was suffering from a bad cold. When he started to sing, it sounded as if another singer had shown up, one whose voice was tight and hard. The experience in Boston terrified Robeson. He became so discouraged that he was seriously considering quitting the concert stage. Essie had another idea together. She convinced Paul to seek out the advice of a professional voice teacher. As a high-school student, Essie had had voice training. One day when they ran into Theresa Armitage, her former voice teacher in New York, it seemed like a good omen.

Robeson complained to Armitage about the limited range of his voice. "You just think your range is short," she told him. "It's all of two and a quarter octaves. . . ." (An octave is a group of eight tones: for instance, C, D, E, F, G, A, B, C.)

"[J]ust open your mouth and throat and let the tone come out freely," she coached him. "Don't *set* your throat—that closes it. Relax it, and you'll see how the voice rolls out. . . . And now, my child, you will always know that you are singing *right* when you do not tire."

Robeson was cheered by other news that spring as well. Four records that he and Larry Brown had made earlier had sold 55,000 copies. Their Negro spirituals were beginning to reach an ever wider audience.

41

That summer Robeson went into rehearsal for a play called *Black Boy*. It was about the life of Jack Johnson, the first black heavyweight boxing champion. Although the play was not well received and closed in a short time, the notices for Robeson were favorable.

Robeson and Brown went back out on the road. This time it was for a concert tour to the Midwest. In February 1927, Paul returned to New York. Essie greeted her husband with the news that they were going to be parents. Paul was on another concert tour of Europe when Paul Robeson Jr., whom they nicknamed "Pauli," was born on November 2, 1927. The birth of his son made Paul feel the need to make a better living.

One thing he considered was singing opera. However, that did not present much of an option. For even when an opera of *The Emperor Jones* was staged by the Metropolitan Opera, the role of Brutus Jones was sung by a white man wearing black makeup.

Another possibility was to perform in musicals and movies. This seemed like a better choice for Paul. Also, Essie could serve as his manager. In March 1928, Robeson sang the role of Crown in the DuBose and Dorothy Heyward musical of *Porgy*. It was the only time that Paul ever played a villain. (*Porgy* turned out to be the forerunner of George Gershwin's 1935 opera *Porgy and Bess*.)

By the next month, Robeson was sailing to London to sing the part of Joe the Riverman in Jerome Kern and Oscar Hammerstein II's *Show Boat*. This "All American Musical Comedy" was in the words of Oscar Hammerstein II, who wrote the lyrics, "big and meant to stay that way." It featured a cast of 160, headed by Captain Andy Hawks (played by the English actor Cedric Hardwicke), who lived and worked on a riverboat, the *Cotton Blossom*. This paddle wheeler steamed up and down the Mississippi River from the 1880s to the 1920s, pulling into river port towns, its calliope blaring, to entertain the local people with singing, dancing, and even gambling.

Robeson would be singing the showstopper, "Ol' Man River." Jerome Kern had even had Paul Robeson in mind when he composed the song and had sent it to him as soon as it was finished. In spite of performing in this musical, he would have ample time to perform concerts with Larry Brown.

Everything went according to plan. *Show Boat* was playing to a packed Theater Royal night after night with Robeson's "Ol' Man River" as the song that wound throughout the performance and served as the musical climax of the evening. As a matter of fact, the most talked about and thrilling moment of the London theater that season was when Robeson set down the bale of cotton he'd been toting, and sang in his rich bass voice:

> Ah gits weary an' sick of try-in',
> Ah'm tired of liv-in' an' skeered of dy-in',
> But ol' man river,
> He jus' keeps roll-in' a-long.

The concerts turned out to be equally successful. James Douglas in the *Daily Express* of July 15, 1928, painted a clear picture of what it was like to spend an evening in the concert hall listening to Paul Robeson:

> Before he sings a note he looks at you with his dream-charged eyes. Then, as you yield to his powerful domination, he turns his head with a smile to Lawrence Brown at the piano, and nods. He has you, and he holds you in a dream-state till the song creeps back into the silence out of which it came. . . .
>
> I have heard all the great singers of our time. No voice has ever moved me so profoundly with so many passions of thought and emotion.

Essie and Paul Robeson were once again enjoying living in London, and Londoners were enjoying having them there. The night the Prince of Wales attended a concert he liked what he heard so much that he scheduled a command performance for the king of Spain. There were dinner parties where they met the playwright and critic George Bernard Shaw, who had won the Nobel Prize for Literature in 1925; the novelist and historian H. G. Wells, who had written *The Time Machine* and *The War of the Worlds*; and the politician and pacifist Ramsay MacDonald, who had been Britain's first Labour prime minister. "I found myself moving a great deal in the most aristocratic circles," said an amazed Robeson. When *Show Boat* closed in March of 1929, the Robesons remained in England. For the next 10 years, much of the time they used London as their headquarters, traveling to countries near and far to present concerts and to work on plays and films.

It was while in Budapest, Hungary, that Robeson was struck by a similarity between Negro spirituals and Russian folk songs. Folk songs are traditional or composed songs, usually in stanzas with refrains and a simple melody. "The Russian has the same rhythmic quality—but not the melodic beauty of the African," he realized. "It is an emotional product, developed, I think, through suffering." Robeson was developing an interest in the folk songs of the world. It was a passion that would last the rest of his musical career.

In April 1930, Paul Robeson began rehearsals to play one of the greatest roles in all of Shakespeare: Othello. Here in the words of Thomas Rymer, a 17th-century critic, is what happens in this play:

> Othello, a Blackmoor Captain, by talking of his Prowess and Feats of War, makes Desdemona a Senators Daughter to be in love with him; and to be married to him, without her Parents knowledge; And having preferred Cassio, to be his Lieutenant, (a place which his Ensign Iago sued for) Iago in revenge, works the Moor into a Jealousy that Cassio Cuckolds him: which he effects by stealing and conveying a certain Handkerchief, which had, at the Wedding, been by the Moor presented to his Bride. Hereupon, Othello and Iago plot the Deaths of Desdemona and Cassio, Othello Murders her, and soon after is convinced of her Innocence. And as he is about to be carried to Prison, in order to be punish'd for the Murder, He kills himself.

Seventy years had passed since the last black man, the much acclaimed Ira Aldrich, had played Othello on the English stage. It was an undertaking that Paul Robeson approached with the dedication of the scholar. Robeson not only studied the play in French, German, Russian, and Yiddish, he read everything he could find about Shakespeare so that he would feel "in touch with the English spirit." As Paul explained to a *New York Times* reporter on May 18, 1930:

> I feel the play is modern, for the problem is the problem of my own people. It is a tragedy of racial conflict, a tragedy of honor rather than of jealousy. . . . The fact that he is an alien among white people makes his mind work more quickly. He feels dishonor more deeply. His color heightens the tragedy.

Paul Robeson immersed himself in the language of Shakespeare's day, so that he would, for instance, be able to use the broad British *A*. He would say *chaunce* rather than *chance*, *demaunde* instead of *demand*.

In addition, because he felt that Othello would move about the stage with the fluid grace of a panther, he frequently visited the London Zoo to study how the panther glided around its cage.

One huge obstacle that the production faced was that its director, Nellie Van Volkenburg, had never directed a Shakespearean play before. Her inexperience and lack of instruction forced the actors to rely on each other. Maurice Browne, who was playing Iago and had contacted Paul about playing the role; Peggy Ashcroft, who was playing Desdemona; Sybil Thorndike as Emilia—all developed a closeness in their need to help each other and even met at each other's apartments to rehearse.

Opening night at the Savoy Theatre was on May 19, 1930. Although the supporting cast was strong, the crowd rose to its feet at the final curtain with cheers of "Robeson!" and "Speech!" At long last, after 20 curtain calls, Robeson came forward to speak. "I took the part of Othello with much fear," Robeson told the audience. "Now I am so happy."

Eight of the 12 opening night reviews were just as appreciative. "There has been no Othello on our stage, certainly for forty years, to compare with his dignity, simplicity and true passion," praised the reviewer for the *Morning Post.* "[O]ne only wishes some of our actors could take example from his rolling and natural response to the rhythm and beauty of Shakespeare's verse."

Robeson became the man of the hour on the English stage. "This has been, in fact, a Robeson day in London," declared the *New York Times.*

Interviewers asked Peggy Ashcroft what it was like to play Desdemona opposite Paul Robeson. "For myself," she replied, "I look on it as a privilege to act with a great artist like Paul Robeson."

Although *Othello* ran for a total of only six weeks, it was for Robeson a profound experience marked by change and excitement. "Othello has taken away from me all kinds of fears, all sense of limitation, and all racial prejudice," realized Robeson. "Othello has opened to me new and wider fields; in a word, Othello has made me free."

Essie Robeson was also experiencing a broadening of her own horizons. For some time, she had been writing, and in 1930, Harper & Brothers published *Paul Robeson, Negro,* the book she had been working on about her husband. Interestingly, she had written her biography in the third person, a point of view that at times created a strange distance. For example, here is her account of the birth of Pauli: "Their son was born on November 2nd, 1927. Essie nearly lost her life in the struggle to bring him into the world." It was almost as if she were writing about someone else.

Another aspect of Paul Robeson's life was that he was drifting away from Essie Robeson toward the many women, including some of the actresses he worked with, who found him attractive.

One time, the Robesons were eating dinner with their friend Marion Griffith when this topic came up. (Essie writes about this incident in her biography.)

Paul said to Marion that his wife "thinks I'm brave and honest and moral, when, as a matter of fact, I'm none of those things."

"You know," said Essie, "we've been married for eight years, and we've never yet agreed about anything."

"Why I can remember time after time in my football career," continued Paul, "when I could have and should have made fine

Paul Robeson stars as Othello and Peggy Ashcroft plays
Desdemona in the London production of Shakespeare's *Othello*.

plays in a pinch, I welched them because I knew I'd get hurt."

"Self-preservation is the first law of nature," offered Essie as an explanation.

"Then there was the money my brother Ben sent me from the army—money I was to use to pay important bills and family debts. I knew the bills and the debts were not particularly urgent, so I occasionally kept a cheque and spent it for myself. It wouldn't have been so bad if he hadn't trusted me so completely, or if I had needed the money."

"I must say I don't like the idea of your doing such things, Paul. . . ," agreed Marion. "But, still, they don't seem to be such awful or criminal mistakes."

The third point, his unfaithfulness to Essie, was harder to talk about. "If I were to admit I am, or had been, what good would it do?" Paul asked. "She'd never believe it."

"Then why worry her?" wondered Marion. Essie remained silent.

"Well, it puts me in such a false position with myself, to have her insist that I'm true and faithful, when I might not be," said Paul. "I wouldn't mind if she wasn't so *sure*. You've no idea how awful it is to go about having her convinced that I'm a little tin god when I'm really far from that."

"Well, darling," answered Essie finally, "if I ever thought there were lapses, I thought of the possible reasons for them, and dismissed them as not lapses at all. But what I am thoroughly convinced of is this: . . . I know that you are faithful to me in the all important spirit of things; that I am the one woman in your life, in your thoughts, in your love."

Although this conversation ended in a friendly manner, the issue remained. And as time went by, it was not at all surprising that the Robesons' marriage was affected. Essie and Paul tried trial separations. Sometimes, they were convinced that they should get a divorce. At other times, however, they believed that they should stay together. Nevertheless, in spite of all their difficulties, they did remain married to each other.

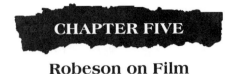

CHAPTER FIVE

Robeson on Film

In mid-1930, Paul Robeson performed in Max Reinhardt's production of *The Emperor Jones* in Berlin, the capital of Germany. Then, in 1931, Paul Robeson appeared in another Eugene O'Neill play, *The Hairy Ape*. He played Yank, a ship stoker, one who shovels coal into the fire to keep the ship's engines going. Because of Robeson's acute laryngitis, however, the play closed after only five performances.

Robeson was exhausted. He had just finished a concert tour before immediately going into rehearsals for the play. His personal life was also filled with indecision about his relationship with his wife. He wound up in bed in a nursing home for a week. It was the first sign of the physical problems that would overwhelm him later in his life.

At the beginning of 1932, Robeson and Brown were off on an American and Canadian concert tour. By this time, Robeson had learned Russian and had added Russian songs to his repertoire. "Certainly many Russian folk songs seem to have come from Negro peasant life," he said. Singing folk songs in their native tongues became one of his major focuses. "I know the wail of the Hebrew and I felt the plaint of the Russian. I understand both, as I do the philosophy of the Chinese, and I feel that both have much in common with the traditions of my own race."

The content of songs was much more in keeping with his interests than was the style. "I have never been much interested in vocal virtuosity," said Robeson. "I have never tried to sing an A-flat while the audience held on to the edge of its collective seat to see if I could make it."

In April, Robeson was again singing the role of Joe the Riverman. This time it was in the American production of *Show Boat*, produced by Florenz Ziegfeld, on New York City's Broadway.

In June, Paul Robeson received what would be his first honorary degree when his alma mater, Rutgers College, awarded him an honorary master of arts degree. By September, he was back in Europe. This time he was alone. Essie and Paul were planning on getting a divorce. "It is all perfectly friendly," remarked Essie, "and we will keep on being friends, but we've seen so much of each other and both are just a bit tired and want our freedom." Furthermore, Robeson was planning to marry Yolande Jackson, a white woman he had met in England. However, all of a sudden Jackson changed her mind when her family threatened to disinherit her. Her family also hastily arranged a marriage for her with a Russian prince.

Shocked by the quick turnabout, Robeson once again plunged himself into work. One of his first projects was playing the part of Jim Harris in the London production of O'Neill's *All God's Chillun Got Wings*. Hitler had just seized power in Germany, and a committee to aid Jewish refugees fleeing the horrors of Nazi Germany contacted the producers of the O'Neill play to ask them to put on a benefit to aid their cause. The English writer H. G. Wells headed the committee. Robeson at first refused to cooperate. "I don't understand politics . . . ," he said. "My province is art." A short time afterward, however he changed his mind. As the years passed, the line between politics and art would all but disappear for Paul Robeson.

By 1932, Robeson had gained worldwide fame.

Paul Robeson at a 1933 recording session. He had begun making phonograph records as early as 1925.

Robeson's career continued with great success at a time when economic conditions were growing steadily worse for most people in the United States and Europe. After the stock market crash of 1929, thousands of businesses had gone bankrupt, many people had lost their life's savings when banks failed, and millions of people were without work. In 1933, during the depths of the Great Depression, one out of four American workers was unemployed. The economic crisis had brought an end to the Harlem Renaissance, but not to Robeson's career. Despite hard times, millions of people went to the movies each week. For a quarter, they could buy a ticket and enjoy a glamorous fantasy, a musical, a comedy, or a gangster film, and for an hour or two they could escape the harsh reality of the Great Depression.

In May 1933, Robeson was back in the United States to act the role of Brutus Jones in the film of O'Neill's *The Emperor Jones.*

This was the first major motion picture in which a Black played the lead and Whites were the supporting actors. Robeson also had it written into his contract that he would not be in a movie that was made on location south of the Mason-Dixon Line, the accepted boundary between the northern and the southern states. Consequently, the tropical island setting was created at Paramount's Astoria Studios on Long Island.

For his six weeks of work, Robeson was paid $15,000; in 1933 that was equal to 15 times the average American factory worker's yearly wages—if that worker was lucky enough to have a factory job. The film was Robeson's first talkie. He had starred in Micheaux's silent movie *Body and Soul* in 1924. The search had been on for actors with good voices ever since talkies had taken over the industry in the late 1920s. Robeson's voice was a real find. But because of the racism of the times, some moviemakers feared that his chief drawback would be the color of his skin.

The first part of the film *The Emperor Jones* shows the rise of Brutus Jones from a simple farmboy to an all-knowing city slicker. Catching his best friend cheating while gambling, Brutus accidentally kills him.

The scene shifts to a chain gang. A white guard tries to force Brutus to strike a fellow prisoner; instead, Brutus hits the white guard and escapes. In the original film version, Brutus kills the white guard; however, the office of Will Hays, the official censor of the movies, did not allow this scene to be shown in the United States. Brutus finds work shoveling coal on a freighter. When the ship gets close to a Caribbean Island, Brutus jumps overboard and swims ashore.

On the island, Brutus is captured by native guards. (It is at this point that Eugene O'Neill's original play began.) Brutus is about to be executed by the island's black leader when a white trader buys him. By means of his intelligence and quick wits, Brutus takes over the white trader's business and then even takes over rule of the island from the black dictator. Brutus takes away the bullets from a gun that is used to shoot him, so that the islanders think of him as a kind of superman. The rest of the film shows the corrupting influence of raw power on Emperor Jones and his subsequent fall from grace.

Paul Robeson was well on his way to becoming a household name in the United States. The National Broadcasting Company asked him to sing on the radio. Millions of Americans were then able to tune in to hear him sing "Water Boy," as well as "Ol' Man River," the song that was fast becoming his musical signature.

After returning to London in August, Robeson and Larry Brown presented more concerts in Great Britain. By this time, Robeson was singing in Finnish, Russian, Spanish, and Welsh. He was also pursuing his interest in Chinese, Arabic, and the African languages of Yoruba, Efik, Benin, and Ashanti. Paul and Essie Robeson even became members of the West African Students'

In 1933, Paul Robeson starred in the film version of Eugene O'Neill's play *The Emperor Jones*.

Union where they met future leaders of Africa, including Kwame Nkrumah of Ghana and Jomo Kenyatta of Kenya.

So, when in the summer of 1934, Alexander Korda, the British movie producer, offered him the lead in *Sanders of the River*, Robeson was excited. He looked forward to playing Bosambo, an African chieftain. He was particularly intrigued by the fact that Zoltan Korda, the director, and a film crew of 15 had spent four months and traveled 15,000 miles to film life in Africa.

Unfortunately, the movie was changed drastically when it was edited. Instead of being an exploration of authentic African life, it retreated into a film about British imperialism. Perhaps the advertising for the film said it all: "A million mad savages fighting for one beautiful woman! . . . until three white comrades ALONE pitched into the fray and quelled the bloody revolt!"

Robeson attended the opening of the film at the Leicester Square Theatre. After the houselights came up, Robeson was asked to make a speech. Instead, he rose and, without saying a word, quickly left the theater.

Black Majesty, a movie being considered by the Russian theater and movie director Sergey Eisenstein, promised to be a far more satisfying project. Eisenstein, who had made such film classics as *The Battleship Potemkin*, now wanted to make a film about Toussaint-Louverture. Toussaint-Louverture was the Haitian patriot who led an overthrow of the French rulers on the island of Haiti. Robeson, when in high school, had won an oratorical contest with his speech about the Haitian general. In December 1934, Essie and Paul, along with their traveling companion the English journalist Marie Seton, set out for Russia to meet with Eisenstein and talk over the possibilities of doing *Black Majesty*.

On the train trip from London to Moscow there was a one-day stopover in Berlin, Germany. The city Robeson had enjoyed four years earlier when he had been in Max Reinhardt's production of *The Emperor Jones* had turned into a frightening place. In 1933, Adolf Hitler had become the chancellor of Germany, and by 1934 he was firmly in power as dictator. The Nazis with their racist and anti-Semitic beliefs had taken over Germany. Hitler's violent storm troopers, known as brownshirts, seemed to be everywhere. And everywhere they seemed to be displeased to see these three travelers. A verbal confrontation with Nazi storm troopers at the Berlin train station threatened to escalate into a physical one. "I figured I could throw two of them onto the tracks and do some damage to two or three more before they got me down," Robeson recalled years later. Barely able to escape as the train was pulling out, Paul Robeson had been shocked by the incident. "I never understood what Fascism was before," he confessed afterward.

It was a great relief when the Robesons and Seton arrived in Moscow, the capital of the Soviet Union (USSR), which consisted of Russia and the old Russian Empire. The Soviet Union included territories inhabited by non-Russians. A problem with their passports detained them at the border until Robeson pulled out a phonograph and played one of his records. Then smiles broke out on the faces of the guards. They knew who Paul Robeson was and greeted him warmly.

The Russian people became even friendlier as soon as Robeson opened his mouth to speak. "I was not prepared for the endless friendliness, which surrounded me from the moment I crossed the border," said Robeson. His Russian was fluent, and the people of Moscow welcomed the travelers with open arms. "Here I am not a Negro but a human being." This would prove to be a defining moment in Robeson's life.

The United States had finally officially recognized the USSR in 1933. However, the American government still opposed the Communist policies put into effect during and after the Russian Revolution of 1917. The Communists had seized private businesses and factories and had put them under government control. By 1924, the Communist political leader Joseph Stalin had made himself dictator. The Soviet Union had just completed its first five-year plan (1928-33). Private farms had been turned into collectives where millions of peasants worked. Conditions on the collectives were terrible for most people. The government slaughtered many farmers during the process of forcing them onto the collectives, and at least 5 million people died in the famine of 1932–33, which collectivization caused. Millions of those who objected to the brutal policies of Stalin were out of sight either in hundreds of slave labor camps or at the bottom of ditches dead by murder or forced starvation.

In contrast to the massive unemployment in the United States and western Europe, the Communists presented the appearance of a workers' paradise where there were jobs and equality for all. The Robesons were provided with comfortable accommodations and many cultural events, such as operas and plays, to attend. They were also taken to showcase hospitals, factories, and child-care centers. The Robesons had never before felt so comfortable among strangers. It was a great contrast to their recent experience in Nazi Germany, as well as to their life in the United States. Frank and John Goode, two of Essie's brothers, also felt the same way, as they were living in Moscow. The Robesons even decided that they wanted their son, Pauli, to go to school in Moscow. As things worked out, Eisenstein and Robeson were never able to coordinate their schedules so that they could make a movie together. After their two-week visit to the Soviet Union, the Robesons returned to England. Robeson went on a concert

During the 1930s, Paul Robeson, accompanied by Lawrence Brown at the piano, performed in many concerts.

tour through England, Scotland, Wales, and Ireland and then appeared in the play *Stevedore* with a cast of nonprofessionals. Robeson played Lonnie Thompson, a dockworker falsely accused of raping a white woman. Thompson dies as he is uniting union workers to withstand the onslaught of a mob.

That same year, 1935, the Robesons had traveled to California, so that Robeson could sing the role of Joe the Riverman in the film version of *Show Boat*. The most satisfying moment of this experience for Robeson came when he had finished singing the last word of "Ol' Man River": the stagehands broke out in applause. For his appearance, Robeson was rewarded with sterling reviews and the princely sum of $40,000.

Paul and Essie Robeson returned to the United States in 1935 so that he could sing in the Hollywood film of *Show Boat.*

Paul Robeson in a scene from the 1935 Hollywood film version of Jerome Kern and Oscar Hammerstein's musical *Show Boat.*

Robeson's next movie, *Song of Freedom,* was made in 1936 and became one of his favorites. "I want to disillusion the world of the idea," said Robeson, "that the Negro is either a stupid fellow or, as the Hollywood superfilms show him, a superstitious savage under the spell of witch doctors."

In *Song of Freedom,* Robeson was cast as a London dockworker named John Zinga. At about the same time that Zinga's wonderful voice is discovered and he becomes an opera star, he also finds out that the medal he wears around his neck proves he is the long-lost king of Casanga. Zinga winds up on a concert tour in order to shore up the finances of his African kingdom.

"Had I been born in Africa," Robeson wrote at the time, "I would have belonged, I hope, to that family which sings and chants the glories and legends of the tribe. I would have liked in my mature years to have been a wise elder, for I worship wisdom and knowledge of the ways of men."

Robeson came to like *Song of Freedom* because it was "the first film to give a true picture of many aspects of the life of the colored man in the West. Hitherto on the screen, he has been caricatured or presented only as a comedy character. This film shows him as a real man." The *Pittsburgh Courier* agreed with this assessment, calling it "the finest story of colored folks yet brought to the screen. . . ."

The second movie Paul Robeson made in 1936, *King Solomon's Mines*, is also about a man who discovers he is a king. Taken from the 1885 novel by Henry Rider Haggard, it is about Allan Quartermaine, a white explorer played by Cedric Hardwicke, who is on his way to Zimbabwe to look for the ancient mines of King Solomon. Robeson played Umbopa, his servant on the expedition, who finds out that he is an African king. After Umbopa takes back his throne, he saves the two white men he once served.

Robeson had studied the African language of Efik in preparation for the role of Umbopa. The similarities between this African language and Chinese led Robeson to discover there were also other similarities, especially in the pentatonic scale theory in music. (The pentatonic scale is a musical scale, like the black keys of the piano, with the fourth and seventh tones omitted. The theory is that it is found in cultures as widely separated as African and Chinese.)

The next film Robeson made was *Big Fella*. The story was taken from *Banjo*, a book by the Jamaican-born American Claude McKay, one of the most militant black writers of the Harlem Renaissance. Banjo, played by Robeson, was a dockworker in the harbor of Marseilles, France. After finding a lost boy and helping him return to his home, Banjo turns down an offer for a different life and returns to the docks. Essie Robeson even had a role in this film as did Robeson's accompanist, Larry Brown.

With the completion of *Big Fella* in 1937, Robeson and Brown embarked on a concert tour of Russia. Before returning to London, the Robesons helped their son Pauli and Essie's mother—Eslanda Goode, who was known as "Ma Goode"—get settled in Moscow. Pauli would be attending a Soviet Model School for two years. Among his classmates would be none other than a daughter of Communist dictator Joseph Stalin. Apparently unknown to the Robesons were the Great Purges that took place in the Soviet Union from 1934 to 1938. Claiming to find political enemies everywhere, Stalin pushed for the trials of Communist Party members and others that resulted in the jailing or the executing of as many as 7 million people.

Shortly after Robeson's return to England, he had started work on another film. *Jericho* (in the United States the film was released as *Dark Sands*) was about Jericho Jackson, played by Paul Robeson, whose medical education has been interrupted by service in World War I. While on board a troopship bound for the

Paul Robeson and his son, Paul Jr., in England in 1936. The Robesons had moved to London in 1928.

fighting in Europe, Jericho Jackson saves the men trapped below deck after the ship is torpedoed. However, there is a white officer who has ordered Jericho Jackson to go above deck; Jackson refuses and helps save more men. Unfortunately, the white officer is accidentally killed, and Jericho Jackson is court-martialed for disobeying an order. He escapes on a lifeboat and drifts to the North African coast. A Captain Mack is court-martialed after being held responsible for Jackson's escape.

Jericho Jackson journeys across the Sahara and meets up with the Tuareg tribe. His medical knowledge cures many of the sick members of the tribe. Jackson eventually marries a Tuareg princess, raises a family, and becomes their leader. He even gets the different nomadic tribes to help each other, rather than fight, during their annual pilgrimage to obtain salt.

Upon hearing of this Tuareg leader, a film crew arrives to make a movie. Back in London, Captain Mack watches this documentary film and realizes that the leader is actually Jericho Jackson. Mack flies to the Sahara to bring Jackson back. However, after observing this respected Tuareg leader in action, Captain Mack changes his mind. He returns without Jericho Jackson.

Not only was this one of the most interesting films that Robeson had made, but it was also the film that he was able to influence the most. The original ending had Captain Mack convincing Jericho Jackson to accompany him back to the United States to stand trial. After taking off, their plane crashes in the desert, killing them both.

Robeson was able to have that ending of the film dropped and replaced by a new conclusion: Captain Mack, returning from Africa alone, dies when his plane crashes. The new message is entirely different from the movie's first version. The original message was that the black man's death is a punishment for violating the white man's system. In the new version, the black man is not killed but instead responds to a higher order of right and wrong.

CHAPTER SIX

A Song to Silence Guns

During the rest of 1937, the Robesons vacationed in the Soviet Union, after which Paul Robeson became involved in international politics by giving concerts in support of the Republican forces in the Spanish Civil War. That brutal war had begun in 1936 with an army revolt in Spanish-controlled Morocco against the Spanish Republic. The fighting had quickly spread to Spain.

Paul Robeson felt that he had to support the Republican side in a war that pitted a democratically elected government against the growing power of racist and dictatorial Nazism and fascism in Europe. The Spanish Republic had been set up with a new constitution in 1931. The new Spanish government's democratically elected parliament forbade the Spanish king, who had left the country, from returning to Spain. It had confiscated the king's property. The new constitution separated church and state, but many Spanish Catholics resented the government's plans to end financial support of their religion, especially of their religious education. For the next five years, a variety of political groups, including Communists, Socialists, left-wing and right-wing Republicans, and moderate and right-wing Catholics ruled in Spain.

But by 1936, the left-wing parties, including the Communists, the Socialists, and the left-wing Republicans, had united to form what they called the Popular Front. The Popular Front won an important election victory over the right-wing Nationalist side, which consisted of conservative Republicans, those wanting the return of the king, Fascists, and those who supported policies of the Catholic Church. When the Popular Front won, it started to put into action a number of controversial social reforms. These included dividing up huge landed estates, forcing factory owners to take back workers whom they had fired because they had gone out on strike, and closing Catholic schools. The army generals leading the revolt against the government promised an end to these policies.

Of special concern to Robeson was the fact that the right-wing forces were led by General Francisco Franco. Mussolini, the dictator of Fascist Italy, sent bombers and between 40,000 and 75,000 Italian troops to help Franco. Even worse, Hitler, dictator of Nazi Germany, sent transport planes, combat planes, tanks, artillery, and about 10,000 pilots and tank troops to help Franco. Official outside support for Spain's democratic government came only from Stalin, dictator of the Soviet Union, who sent some tanks, aircraft, and military advisers.

The Republican side in the Spanish Civil War was partially composed of and supported by Communists. Partly because of that, the United States, Great Britain, and France did not help the Spanish Republic but instead remained neutral in the war. Nevertheless, many citizens of those and other countries joined in voluntary military units called the International Brigades to help the Republican army. For example, the British writer George Orwell (he wrote about the war in *Homage to Catalonia* and later wrote *Animal Farm* and *1984*), French writer André Malraux, and American writer Ernest Hemingway (he later wrote *For Whom the Bell Tolls* and won the Nobel Prize for Literature) fought for the Republican side. Pablo Picasso, the Spanish-born painter who was then living in France, painted his famous *Guernica*, to commemorate the death of hundreds of innocent civilians killed by German terror bombing. Many of these artists and writers were regarded as troublemakers for involving themselves in the struggle against fascism in the Spanish Civil War.

Although Robeson was singing at pro-Spanish Republican rallies, even at the huge Christmas 1937 rally at Albert Hall in London, he did not think he was doing enough for the cause. He wanted to see Spain for himself. So in January 1938, the Robesons crossed over from France into Spain. Wherever they went—Barcelona, Benicasim, Albacete, Tarazona, Madrid—the soldiers were amazed to see this singer and actor whom they had only listened to on records or seen in movies.

"You don't get people like that every day of the week running

Robeson visits Spain in 1938 to sing for soldiers fighting against
Nazi supported Fascist troops in the Spanish Civil War.

into a war to see how things are going," said a sergeant at one of
the hospitals where Robeson sang. Robeson met with troops of
the International Brigades, including men in the integrated
American contingent, the Abraham Lincoln Brigade. This journey
made a big impact on Robeson. He was to look back on his visit
to Spain as "a major turning point" in his life. The trip's highlight
for Robeson occurred on the front lines in Teruel when fighting
briefly stopped. Soldiers on both sides set aside their weapons to
listen to the singer they referred to as Pablito. And when he came
to the line in "Ol' Man River" that went "I'm tired of livin', and
feared of dyin'," Robeson instead sang, "I must keep fightin', until
I'm dying." That was the way he sang it because that was the way
he felt.

Back in London, the Robesons arranged for Ma Goode and
Pauli to leave the Soviet Union where Pauli had been going to

school. That was because a major war in Europe seemed more and more likely. As early as 1935, Nazi Germany had announced a build-up in its army. In 1935, Fascist Italy had invaded the African nation of Ethiopia and within seven months proclaimed the annexation of that country. In 1936, Nazi Germany had reoccupied the Rhineland, which had been taken away from Germany's direct control as a result of Germany's defeat in World War I. In 1938, Germany had taken over part of Czechoslovakia.

In London, Robeson began rehearsals for *Plant in the Sun,* a working-class drama written by Ben Bengal. In it, black workers and white ones participate in a sit-down strike, a new method of protest developed by labor unions during the Great Depression. In a sit-down strike, workers stop working but remain in their place of work. By occupying the factory or workshop, the workers try to force the business owners to give in to their demands for higher pay or better working conditions. Except for Robeson, who played a union organizer, and the director, Herbert Marshall, the cast and crew were made up of nonprofessional actors. As these workers had to make a living, rehearsals could only be held at night or on weekends. Not only was Robeson appearing without charge, he also captivated the other actors with his engaging and unpretentious personality.

During its one-month run, *Plant in the Sun* became the show to see in London. One night Jawaharlal Nehru was in the audience. The Robesons soon became friends with this future prime minister of India who was at that time the leader of Indian protests against British colonial rule of his country.

Next, Robeson and Brown went on a concert tour of Great Britain, where working-class people greeted them with enthusiasm. Once the tour was over, Robeson decided to sing on the stage of London movie theaters for only a fraction of his standard concert fee. More and more, Robeson wanted to sing for the blue-coveralled crowd at sixpence per ticket rather than sing for those wearing gowns and tuxedos who paid pounds sterling.

A little over a year after Robeson had sung to troops in Spain with such high hopes for a Republican victory, the Nationalist forces led by General Francisco Franco had taken complete control of Spain. Hundreds of thousands of people had been killed and hundreds of thousands more had fled from the brutal dictatorship. In April 1939, a few days after the capital city of Madrid surrendered to Franco, the United States recognized the dictatorship as the official, legal government of Spain. The failure of the western democracies to come to the aid of a freely elected government seemed to be a signal to the European dictators that they would be able to take over other countries with little or no military opposition. Almost immediately, Franco announced his support of an anti-Communist agreement already signed by Nazi Germany, Fascist Italy, and Imperial Japan. That same spring, Germany took over the rest of Czechoslovakia and Italy invaded and conquered Albania.

As threats of a major war grew more ominous, Robeson went to Wales to film the movie that was to become his all-time personal favorite, *The Proud Valley*. In this film, Robeson plays a mine worker first and a black man second.

Based on a true story, this film portrays David Goliath, an African American from West Virginia who goes to England to become a dockworker. Before long, high unemployment sends Goliath packing for Wales to work in the coal mines of the Rhondda Valley. Goliath fits right in, helping the miners fight for better working conditions as well as lifting their spirits with his voice. In the end, Goliath gives his life to save his fellow miners.

The Proud Valley is one movie where Robeson's singing comes across as natural. The Welsh people enjoy a long history of singing, so it does not seem out of place. Also, the film displays a heightened sense of realism. Much of the movie was filmed with extras—people hired to act in group scenes—from the village of Mardy and in the actual homes of workers.

After 11 years in London, the Robesons were beginning to feel the need to return home to the United States. One major reason, of course, was that the world seemed to be on the brink of war. In August 1939, the Communist-controlled Soviet Union signed a pact of nonaggression with its enemy Nazi Germany. Each side promised not to attack the other. With that threat of military opposition from the Soviet Union removed, Germany began to menace its neighbor Poland. The other reason for the Robesons' returning to the United States was more personal. "Having helped on many fronts," said Robeson, "I feel that it is now time for me to return to the place of my origin—to those roots which, though imbedded in Negro life, are essentially American. . . ."

The Robesons—Essie, Paul, and Pauli—along with Ma Goode returned to New York City in October 1939 and moved into an apartment in Harlem. World War II had begun the previous month when Germany had attacked Poland. Because Poland had a treaty with France and Great Britain, those nations declared war on Germany. In the meantime, the Soviet Union attacked Poland from the east, and within a few weeks, the German and Soviet governments had divided up and taken over all of Poland. Most Americans favored Great Britain and France but wanted the United States to keep out of the war. Congress quickly passed the Neutrality Act of 1939, which kept the United States neutral but allowed the selling of war supplies to the British and the French.

Under these heightened international tensions, one of the first projects that Robeson undertook in the United States was to sing Norman Corwin's 11-minute "Ballad for Americans." With words by John LaTouche and music by Earl Robinson, it was a patriotic hymn for a patriotic time.

Six hundred people crowded into a theater at the Columbia Broadcasting Company on November 5, 1939. The host, actor Burgess Meredith, introduced the radio show. "Democracy is a good thing," Meredith said. "It works. It may creak a bit, but it works. And in its working, it still turns out good times, good news, good people. . . . Life, liberty, and the pursuit of happiness—of these we sing!"

Then Paul Robeson began to sing:

> Are you an American?
> Am I an American?
> I'm just an Irish, Negro, Jewish, Italian,
> French, and English, Spanish, Russian,
> Chinese, Polish, Scotch, Hungarian,
> Litvak, Swedish, Finnish, Canadian,
> Greek, and Turk, and Czech
> and double-Czech American.

With the words of "Our Country's strong, our Country's young/And her greatest songs are still unsung" ringing in their ears, the studio audience burst into applause that went on for 20 minutes.

It was a patriotic high point for the newly returned Robeson. He even recorded this ballad for Victor Records. Now anyone who had missed hearing him sing "Ballad for Americans" on the radio had another chance. The record became a best-seller.

In January of 1940, Robeson played the title role in *John Henry* on Broadway. He had refused to open the play in Washington, D.C., when he learned that the theater there had racially segregated seating for the audience. Although the

A 1943 radio broadcast of "Ballad for Americans." Robeson had thrilled millions of radio listeners when he first sang it in 1939.

Broadway play lasted only five performances, the *New York Times* drama critic Brooks Atkinson paid the actor special tribute:

> It serves chiefly to renew acquaintance with a man of magnificence who ought to be on the stage frequently in plays that suit him. For there is something heroic about this huge man with the deep voice and a great personal dignity. Count as one of the theatre's extravagances the fact that Paul Robeson is not an active figure in it.

That same month, the Herbert Hoover Relief Fund scheduled a benefit to aid Finnish citizens. During the fall of 1939, the Soviet Union had attacked Finland in order to gain territory that it wanted to use for military bases. Stalin, the dictator of the Soviet Union, realized that once Germany had digested its conquests it would probably break the nonaggression treaty and attack the Soviet Union. Stalin wanted the bases so that the Soviet Union would be militarily prepared. Although Paul Robeson was invited to the benefit, he refused to appear. He said he could not be sure that the news accounts about the Soviet Union were accurate. After all, he reasoned, newspapers in the past had reported things that were untrue.

Robeson was criticized for favoring the Soviet Union's attack on its little neighbor Finland. Some conservative people began to consider Robeson a troublemaker. After all, hadn't Robeson supported the Communist-dominated International Brigades in Spain? Hadn't he protested long-established racial segregation in the South by refusing to perform there? Hadn't he starred in roles glorifying labor unions that went out on strike against their employers? And hadn't he spoken at rallies supporting labor unions?

Nevertheless, Robeson's popularity continued to grow. Two months after the Finland benefit incident, Hamilton College in New York State presented Robeson—this "student, athlete, lawyer, actor, singer and great American"—with an honorary degree. After honoring Paul Robeson by draping the hood of Doctor of Humane Letters over him, the president of the college, Dr. W. H . Cowley, spoke to him before the commencement audience:

> We honor you chiefly as a man—a man of tremendous stature, energy and physical dexterity; a man of brilliant mind, a man whose sensitive spirit makes possible your penetrating interpretations; and a man who, above all else, travels across the world as an example of the humanity and the greatness of our democratic heritage.

That summer, Robeson again sang the "Ballad for Americans." One concert was for an audience of 160,000 in Chicago's Grant Park; another was for 30,000 people at the Hollywood Bowl in Los Angeles. Yet even though he was a famous star, Robeson experienced racial discrimination in hotels and restaurants in cities such as New York, San Francisco, and Los Angeles.

In the spring of 1941, the Robesons bought a 12-room home on a two-and-a-half-acre estate in Enfield, Connecticut. Set among tall trees, the Georgian colonial house and grounds featured a billiards room, a bowling alley, and a swimming pool. Called "The Beeches," it was a place away from the city, a place that Essie and Pauli grew to love. Essie even had a darkroom installed so that she could develop her own photographs. Paul, however, still spent most of his time in New York City.

During the period from 1939 to mid-1941, when the Soviet Union and Nazi Germany were honoring their nonaggression pact, Robeson criticized Great Britain's fight against Germany. He said that it was foolish to think that the British were fighting to defend democracy when they oppressed black people in their colonies and would not allow India to be independent. This angered many Americans who had been horrified when German armies invaded and occupied other European countries and when German planes bombed British cities. Then, in June 1941, came Germany's long-expected invasion of the Soviet Union. Great Britain immediately promised aid to the Soviet Union. The United States, although officially neutral, nevertheless, signed an agreement with the Soviet Union. It promised to supply that

Communist country with needed war supplies. The United States even made a billion dollars available to the Soviet Union so that it could afford to buy these supplies. Robeson then wholeheartedly supported the British and American war efforts.

In September of 1941, Paul Robeson spoke before a crowd of 20,000 at Madison Square Garden in New York City. "Let us start off with a couple of songs that mean a lot to me and I know mean a lot to you—just a few phrases from the 'Bill of Rights.'" It was a rally to free Earl Browder, the head of the U.S. Communist Party. Browder, the Communist presidential candidate in the 1936 and 1940 elections, had been sentenced to four years in jail for passport irregularities.

Earlier in 1941, J. Edgar Hoover, the director of the Federal Bureau of Investigation (FBI), had opened up an investigation of Robeson's political activities. The FBI began labeling Robeson as

Paul, Essie, and Paul Jr. at home at "The Beeches," their Enfield, Connecticut, estate in the early 1940s.

Paul Robeson, Eleanor Roosevelt (the President's wife), and actress Helen Hayes at a 1942 "Salute to Negro Troops" pageant.

a member of the Communist Party. By the following year, Robeson's telephone was being tapped, and agents were frequently following him around.

Robeson was certainly becoming more political both off and on the stage. Robeson spoke at rallies supporting the Soviet Union. This became more acceptable to most Americans after the United States entered World War II in December 1941. After all, the Soviet Union was now a very important American ally. Throughout the war, Robeson performed and spoke out at war bond rallies and at benefit concerts for war refugees. He also recorded programs broadcast to American and Allied troops. He increased his activities, fighting what he believed were serious injustices, even if his actions sometimes made people consider him to be a troublemaker. In the middle of a concert in 1942 in Kansas City, Missouri, Robeson told the audience of his outrage when he realized that, despite preconcert promises to him, all the African Americans had to sit in the balcony. He said he was continuing the concert, but only under protest. In Santa Fe, New Mexico, Robeson refused to perform at a concert because a Santa Fe hotel would not honor his hotel reservation because he was an African American.

In 1942, Robeson also made his last major movie. It was called *Tales of Manhattan* and featured some of the biggest names in Hollywood: Henry Fonda, Rita Hayworth, Charles Laughton, Edward G. Robinson, Cesar Romero, Ginger Rogers, and Ethel Waters. The plot spins around an old overcoat filled with thousands of dollars and how it affects all the different people who find it. Two of those who pick up this money are a sharecropper and his wife, played by Paul Robeson and Ethel Waters.

"It was the same old thing," complained Robeson, "the Negro solving his problem by singing his way to glory. This is very offensive to my people. It makes the Negro childlike and innocent and is in the old plantation tradition."

From that time on, Robeson vowed only to get involved with projects that he felt were worth doing. His next undertaking was narrating and singing for a documentary movie about civil rights called *Native Land*, which was shown in 1942.

Four years earlier, the U.S. House of Representatives had set up the Committee on Un-American Activities to investigate Communist influence in various organizations. Martin Dies, the chairman of the House Committee on Un-American Activities, said that the film *Native Land* was based on the African American writer Richard Wright's book of the same name. Actually, while Wright was sympathetic to the Communist cause, the movie had nothing to do with his novel, which was entitled *Native Son*. Nevertheless, this was the beginning of the notion of guilt by association, something that would reach its height during the McCarthy years of the early 1950s.

CHAPTER SEVEN

"The Fortunes of the Moor"

More than 10 years had passed since Robeson had played Othello. During that time he had grown both as a person and as an actor, and he now felt ready again for the challenges of the role. Rehearsals began under Margaret Webster, an experienced director who would also play the part of Emilia. José Ferrer and his wife, Uta Hagen, would perform in the roles of Iago and Desdemona.

Othello opened in Cambridge, Massachusetts, to very good reviews. However, it was another 14 months before the production would open in New York City.

With six weeks remaining before the Broadway opening on October 19, 1943, rehearsals began. This became a difficult time for Robeson. He felt that he had not been good enough in the 1930 production. Margaret Webster, the director, had seen the first *Othello* and agreed with his assessment.

Looking back on his life in the theater, Robeson realized that he had received very little instruction. Under James Light's direction at the Provincetown Theater, the belief had been that it was not good to tamper with Robeson's natural acting ability. And the director of the 1930 production of *Othello*, Nellie Van Volkenburg, had been too inexperienced to offer any guidance whatsoever.

What Robeson most needed to develop in his characterization of Othello was his sense of rage. After listening carefully to the director, consulting Shakespearean scholars, and thinking about it himself, Robeson finally decided the way he would do it.

Robeson came to the conclusion that "Othello kills not in hate but in honor." When Desdemona seems to be unfaithful to him (of course, it is actually Iago's treachery that leads him to think so), "it was the destruction of himself as a human being, of his human dignity."

With this in mind, Robeson was able to lay out a way to portray Othello. "The way I play it, I'm calm, I'm quiet, through all the early part," said Robeson. "I don't make an unnecessary move. And I think that's right. Of course, if I didn't have a mighty active Iago, I couldn't get away with that massive calmness, perhaps, but with Joe [José Ferrer] all over the stage the way he is, it is an effective contrast."

Robeson's portrayal of Othello also coincided with his reading of the historical period. "Othello came from a culture as great as that of ancient Venice," explained Robeson. "He came from an Africa of equal stature. And he felt he was betrayed. He felt his honor was betrayed and his human dignity was betrayed."

Robeson could also pattern his portrayal of Othello after his own life. It was that same sense of dignity that his father had possessed and had instilled in his son. It was the sense of self that had made Paul Robeson seek and attain the best grades at Rutgers. It was the force that drove him not only to overcome major obstacles to make the football team but also to attain All-American honors.

Practicing the role of Othello was so demanding that after a full day of rehearsing the exhausted Robeson would need to sleep for 12 hours. What had attracted him to this role? It had certainly not been the money. He could make over $2,000 for a single concert; whereas, for a whole week of *Othello* his salary was $1,500. Nor had it been for the aggrandizement of his ego. Robeson was just another member of the cast. This was in evidence one day when the *Othello* cast and crew played a softball game in Manhattan's Central Park. The other show team joked that the *Othello* team's heavy hitter was not really Paul Robeson. "If I'm not Paul Robeson," he shot back, "I learned all those lines for nothing." Robeson's team went on to win 24 to 3.

Robeson's real reason for playing Othello was bigger than himself. "Not simply for art's sake do I try to excel in *Othello*," he explained, "but more to prove the capacity of the people from whom I've sprung and of all such peoples, of whatever color, erroneously regarded as backward."

The opening night at the Shubert Theatre proved to be a roaring success. When the curtain rang down on the final act, the audience clapped for 20 minutes. October 19, 1943, would become the night that "the doors of the American theatre opened for the Negro people."

The softball game in Central Park had just been a warm-up for the baseball owners' meeting that winter when Paul Robeson spoke to the commissioner of baseball, Kenesaw Mountain Landis, as well as to the owners. "I come here as an American and former athlete," Robeson said to them. He then spoke for 20 minutes about the need to end the color barrier in major-league baseball.

"I can understand the owners' fears that there would be trouble if Negroes were to play in the big leagues," wrote Robeson later, "but my football experience showed me such fears are groundless. Because baseball is a national game, it is up to baseball to see that discrimination does not become the American pattern."

The United States in 1943 was in the midst of war with the racist Nazis. Yet not only were the U.S. armed forces still racially segregated, but on the home front, major-league baseball, the most popular American sport, was still played with all-white teams. Nevertheless, Robeson had opened another crack in the dam that would break four years later when Branch Rickey, the general manager of the Brooklyn Dodgers, inserted Jack Roosevelt "Jackie" Robinson into the lineup after having him play in the minor leagues for two years.

The reviewers' praise kept *Othello* on Broadway for 296 consecutive performances, breaking the record for a Shakespearean production. (The previous record had been 157 performances for Orson Welles's *Julius Caesar*.)

Robeson's popularity was further shown by the birthday party that was given for him in New York City in April of 1944. Eight thousand people showed up at the 17th Regiment Armory on Park Avenue to serenade Robeson with Happy Birthday.

When the 10-month run on Broadway was over, *Othello* toured Canada and the United States. *Othello* played in 45 cities, everywhere except in the South. After Robeson's experience in Kansas City, he would not sing or act in any theaters that were segregated. Nevertheless, after the show was over, Robeson did have to return to the real world. Although he could entertain anyone, Robeson could not eat in certain restaurants nor stay in some hotels—the reason was their policies of discrimination against African Americans.

In April, when *Othello* finally closed in Chicago, more than 500,000 people had seen Robeson as the Moor. "Through my performance of Othello I have been able to reach people who would never listen to me if I was in some other field," said Robeson. He had also been awarded the New York Newspaper Guild's Page One Award, the Donaldson Award for Outstanding Lead Performance in 1944, and the American Academy of Arts and Letters medal for best diction on the American stage. The American *Othello* would prove to be the high point of Robeson's acting career, as well as the peak of his popularity.

On April 12, 1945, President Franklin D. Roosevelt died. Shortly afterward, Robeson read a poem by Carl Sandburg in honor of the President before a meeting of the Independent Citizens' Committee of the Arts, Sciences and Professions. "The art of the man is still now," read Robeson. "Yet his shadow lingers alive and speaking/To the whole family of man round the earth."

Robeson himself received many more honors, including honorary degrees from Morehouse College in Atlanta, Georgia, and from Howard University in Washington, D.C. He was also awarded the Spingarn Medal, presented by the NAACP for the year's highest achievement by a black American.

In 1945, World War II finally ended with the defeat of Germany and Japan and the victory of the Allies. The United States and the Soviet Union were now the world's two superpowers. Not long after the end of World War II, the situation between the Western democracies and the Communist-run Soviet Union worsened. Soviet-supported Communists had seized power in most Eastern European countries.

On March 5, 1946, the former British prime minister Winston Churchill gave a name to what was happening in a speech at Fulton, Missouri. "From Stettin [Poland] in the Baltic to Trieste [Italy] in the Adriatic," said Churchill, "an iron curtain has descended across the continent [of Europe]." Churchill set the scene with an image, the Iron Curtain, which turned into a solid reality as the two superpowers grew further and further apart. This growing conflict between the mostly democratic and capitalist Western nations and the politically unfree Soviet Union and the Communist countries it controlled came to be called the cold war. It did not involve direct military action between the United States and the Soviet Union, but it did include economic, political, and military rivalry and mistrust. For example, soon after the United States demonstrated its military might by dropping atomic bombs on Japan in 1945, the Soviet Union speeded up its own program to develop nuclear weapons.

The United States faced not only international conflict. At home, violence toward Blacks had been increasing. During a 15-month period in 1945 and 1946, a total of 56 Blacks had been killed in lynchings. In lynchings, people who are accused of a crime are put to death without the normal legal processes to determine guilt. In the past, an angry mob might beat, torture, mutilate, shoot, burn or hang the victim until dead, all done without any trial to determine if the accused was guilty or not. Between 1882 and 1962, in the United States 4,736 people were lynched, three out of four of them African Americans. Although the peak years for lynching had been in the 1890s, it seemed to be increasing again.

In September, Robeson spoke out against racial violence at a rally in Madison Square Garden. "This swelling wave of lynch murders and mob assaults against Negro men and women," said Robeson, "represents the ultimate limit of bestial brutality to which the enemies of democracy, be they German-Nazis or American Ku Kluxers, are ready to go in imposing their will."

On September 23, 1946, Robeson led a delegation of the Anti-Lynching Crusade to Washington, D.C., to meet with President Truman. The *New York Times* reported that the "President, according to Mr. Robeson, indicated that political matters made it difficult to issue a statement of his views at this time."

On October 7, 1946, Robeson appeared before the state of California's Tenney Committee on Un-American Activities. Robeson was called because of his association with groups that the committee believed were pro-Communist. Under direct questioning Robeson was asked: "But are you a member of the Communist Party?"

It was one of the very few times that he would answer this

78

question directly. "As far as I know," Robeson said, "the Communist Party is a very legal one in the United States. I sort of characterize myself as an anti-Fascist and independent. If I wanted to join any party, I could just as conceivably join the Communist Party, more so today, than I could join the Republican or Democratic Party. But I am not a Communist."

Politics was beginning to play a larger part in Robeson's life. At the end of a concert in March of 1947 at the University of Utah in Salt Lake City, Robeson sang the ballad of "Joe Hill":

> I dreamed I saw Joe Hill last night,
> Alive as you and me.
> Says I, "But Joe you're ten years dead,"
> "I never died," says he. . . .

Nowadays this song may be a part of the repertoire of many folksingers, but in the late 1940s it was considered a radical song to sing, especially in the state of Utah. There the mining companies had long opposed having their workers join labor unions that would demand higher wages and better working conditions.

Joe Hill, a Swedish-born American songwriter and union organizer, had been sentenced to death 32 years earlier in Utah after a trial for murder. Many of Hill's friends and supporters, however, said that he had not committed the crime. They claimed that Joe Hill had been framed by the copper

Singers Lena Horne and Paul Robeson prepare for a 1946 rally at Madison Square Garden.

mining companies. Despite large protest demonstrations and even an appeal from President Woodrow Wilson, the Utah governor ordered Hill's execution by firing squad to proceed. After his execution, "Joe Hill" had become a rallying cry for unions and oppressed workers. Ten years after Hill's death, the famous ballad of "Joe Hill" was written.

After Robeson finished singing the song, the audience sat in silence, stunned that anyone would dare sing this song in Utah. Then Robeson made the following announcement: "You've heard my final concert for at least two years and perhaps for many more. I'm retiring here and now from concert work—I shall sing from now on, for my trade union and college friends; in other words, only at gatherings where I can sing what I please."

On May 31, 1948, Robeson was questioned by the House Un-American Activities Committee and the Senate Committee hearings on the Mundt-Nixon Bill. The first provision of this bill stated: "That all Communist Party members register, be declared ineligible for Federal Employment, be denied passports, and be subject to immediate deportation if aliens."

When the Senate Committee asked Robeson if he were a Communist, Robeson responded, "Some of the most brilliant and distinguished Americans are about to go to jail for failure to answer that question and I am going to join them, if necessary. I refuse to answer the question."

Although the House of Representatives had passed the Mundt-Nixon bill by a vote of 319 to 58 with 34 abstentions, the Senate bowed to the mounting pressure opposing it and did not even bring it up for a vote.

Newspaper reporters began routinely asking Robeson if he was a Communist. Robeson would often answer that he was anti-Fascist. And one time in response to a question as to whether or not he believed in turning the other cheek, he replied: "If someone hit me on one cheek, I'd tear his head off before he could hit me on the other one."

From April to August 1948, Robeson campaigned on behalf of Henry A. Wallace, the Progressive Party's candidate for President of the United States. Robeson was so effective a campaigner that at one point he was even briefly considered as the Progressive

Robeson protests segregation at a Washington, D.C., theater.
Behind him is Earl Robinson, composer of "Ballad for Americans."

Party's candidate for Vice-President of the United States. (The folksinger and political activist Pete Seeger once remarked, "In a truly democratic America, Robeson would have been president.") Robeson quickly discouraged any thoughts about his entry into politics.

Henry A. Wallace, who had been secretary of agriculture and Vice-President in the administrations of President Franklin D. Roosevelt, had been dropped as secretary of commerce by President Harry S. Truman when Wallace opposed Truman's tough stance on the Soviet Union. Two features of the Progressive Party's platform were to promote equal rights for all Americans and to better relations with the Soviet Union.

In November 1948, Harry S. Truman of the Democratic Party defeated Thomas E. Dewey of the Republican Party by a vote of 24 million to 22 million. Although the Progressive Party came in a distant fourth with only slightly more than 1 million votes, this third party had forced Truman and the Democrats to become more liberal than they otherwise would have been.

As might have been anticipated, there was a negative reaction to Robeson's involvement with the Progressive Party. Many people branded the group Communists. The Transport Workers Union did not invite Robeson to their convention that year, even though he had been a guest for the 10 previous years. A more serious blow to Paul Robeson's career was the cancellation of the American concerts that had been scheduled for the 1949-50 season.

In February 1949, the Robesons journeyed to London for another concert tour. "I decided to go to Europe to resume my professional concerts," reasoned Robeson. "I wanted to make it perfectly clear that the world is wide and a few pressures could not stop my career."

Robeson quickly found out that in Europe he was still as popular as ever. For his concert in Manchester, England, 10,000 tickets were sold in just a matter of hours. His two concerts at the Albert Hall in London were also sold out.

In April 1949, Robeson flew to Paris for the World Peace

Robeson and scientist Albert Einstein supported Progressive Party presidential candidate Henry A. Wallace (on the left).

Paul Robeson, shown here in Oregon, lost much of his popularity when he toured the country in support of the Progressive Party.

Congress. Although he was only one of 20,000 delegates from 50 nations around the world, he was slated to be one of the featured speakers. On April 21, 1949, a passionate Robeson stood before the assembly and delivered a fateful speech.

As quoted by the Associated Press, the words Robeson supposedly said were printed in newspapers across the United States. Here is what it was reported he said:

> We colonial peoples have contributed to the building of the United States and are determined to share in its wealth. We denounce the policy of the United States government, which is similar to that of Hitler and Goebbels. We want peace and liberty and will combat for them along with the Soviet Union, the democracies of eastern Europe, China and Indonesia. . . .
>
> It is unthinkable that American Negroes could go

83

to war on behalf of those who have oppressed us for generations against a country [the Soviet Union] which in one generation has raised our people to the full dignity of mankind. . . .

Tragically for Robeson, no one at the time bothered to check the accuracy of the quotations, and the damage was done.

The newspaper accounts created a shock wave for many politicians in Washington, D.C., and a firestorm of protest from many U.S. citizens. No longer would Robeson be pointed to as an example of what an African American could accomplish in the United States, nor would he be remembered for his patriotic singing and support of democratic causes. Robeson would from now on be routinely regarded as a traitor. Some even thought him to be the enemy.

An editorial in the *New York Times* echoed the thoughts of many when it lamented that Robeson should "devote his life to making speeches. . . . We want him to sing, and to go on being Paul Robeson."

After the World Peace Congress incident, Robeson sang to huge crowds in Norway and Sweden. But even in a liberal place such as Sweden, Robeson heard boos for the first time when he sang a song about communism. On May 2, 1949, Robeson commented that "what I said has been distorted out of all recognition." He went on to tell the reporter from a Danish newspaper that the "emphasis in what I said in Paris was on the struggle for peace, not on anybody going to war against anybody."

After three concerts in the Soviet Union, the Robesons returned to the United States. They were unsure of what to expect back home.

On June 19, 1949, Paul Robeson Jr. (Pauli), a recent graduate in electrical engineering from Cornell University, married Marilyn Paula Greenberg, a classmate. Although these 21-year-olds had a private ceremony at the minister's apartment, outside in the streets waited hundreds of people. Many were yelling insults directed toward the black groom and the white bride.

After the ceremony, one press photographer even followed the father of the groom into his taxicab. "I have the greatest contempt for the democratic press," said Paul Robeson to the photographer, "and there is something within me keeps me from smashing your cameras over your heads."

Later that evening, Paul Robeson spoke at a Welcome Home Rally held at the Rockland Palace in Harlem.

"It is especially moving to be here in this particular auditorium in Harlem," Robeson told the crowd of 4,500. "Way back in 1918, I came here to this very hall from a football game at the Polo Grounds between Rutgers and Syracuse. . . . I was then, through my athletics and my university record, trying to hold up the prestige of my people; trying in the only way I knew to ease the path for future Negro boys and girls. And I am still in there slugging, yes, at another level, and you can bet your life that I shall battle every step of the way until conditions around these corners change and conditions change for the Negro people all up and down this land."

That evening Paul Robeson went on to issue a challenge. "I defy any part of an insolent, dominating America, however powerful," he said, "I defy any errand boys, Uncle Toms of the Negro people, to challenge my Americanism, because by word and deed I challenge this vicious system to the death; because I refuse to let my personal success, as part of a fraction of one per cent of the Negro people,

Robeson delivering his controversial 1949 speech at the World Peace Congress in Paris.

Paul Robeson meets the world-famous educator, scholar, and writer W. E. B. Du Bois at the 1949 World Peace Congress.

explain away the injustices to fourteen million of my people; because with all the energy at my command, I fight for the right of the Negro people and other oppressed labor-driven Americans to have decent homes, decent jobs, and the dignity that belongs to every human being!"

And then in a variation on his speech at the World Peace Congress in Paris, Robeson said: "For any kind of decent life we need, we want, and *we demand* our constitutional rights—RIGHT HERE IN AMERICA. We do not want to die in vain any more on foreign battlefields for Wall Street and the greedy supporters of domestic fascism. If we must die, let it be in Mississippi or Georgia! Let it be wherever we are lynched and deprived of our rights as human beings!"

The next day the article covering the rally in the *New York Times* was topped by a headline of "Loves Soviet Best, Robeson Declares."

In July, the House Un-American Activities Committee held hearings at which people testified against Robeson. The commit-

86

tee had the power to investigate charges that organizations or people were Communists. Unlike a court of law, however, those accused did not have the right to cross-examine accusers or refute accusations. At widely publicized public hearings, committee members often demanded that witnesses provide the names of Communists. The most prominent speaker at the July hearings was Jackie Robinson, the Brooklyn Dodger great and the first African American ballplayer in major-league baseball. Not only was this difficult for Jackie Robinson because as a young man he had idolized Robeson, but also because Paul Robeson had earlier protested the lack of any black ballplayers in major-league baseball to the commissioner of baseball.

"I've been asked to express my views on Paul Robeson's statement in Paris to the effect that American Negroes would refuse to fight in any war against Russia because we love Russia so much...," said Jackie Robinson to the committee, reading from a prepared statement. "[H]e has a right to his personal views, and if he wants to sound silly when he expresses them in public, that's his business and not mine. He's still a famous ex-athlete and a great singer and actor." But Robinson also had this to say, "[T]he fact that it is a Communist who denounces injustice in the courts, police brutality, and lynching when it happens doesn't change the truth of his charges...."

The anti-Robeson sentiment that was quickly building reached a hysterical and violent climax at two concerts in the late summer of 1949 near the small city of Peekskill, New York.

CHAPTER EIGHT

"A Prisoner in His Native Land"

On August 27, 1949, a Paul Robeson benefit concert was scheduled for the Lakeland Acres picnic grounds, three miles outside of Peekskill, New York. The proceeds from this concert would go to the Harlem chapter of the Civil Rights Congress.

Although this was the fourth summer in a row that Paul Robeson had performed a concert in the area, it was the first one since he had received all the unfavorable publicity of that spring and summer.

The local newspaper, the Peekskill *Evening Star,* ran a front-page headline: "Robeson Concert Here Aids 'Subversive' Unit—Is Sponsored by 'People's Artists' Called Red Front in California." The U.S. attorney general had listed the Civil Rights Congress as a subversive group.

Inside this edition of the *Evening Star* was an editorial that declared the following:

> It appears that Peekskill is to be treated to another concert visit by Paul Robeson. . . . As things stand today, like most folks who put America first, we're a little doubtful of that honor. . . .
>
> [This concert will] consist of an unsavory mixture of song and political talk by one who has described Russia as his "second motherland" and who has avowed "the greatest contempt" for the democratic press. . . . The time for tolerant silence that signifies approval is running out.

Vincent Boyle, the commander of the local American Legion post, wrote a letter that appeared in the August 23 *Evening Star.*

> The present days seem to be crucial ones for resi-

dents of this area with the present epidemic of polio. Now we are being plagued with another, namely, the appearance of Paul Robeson and his Communistic followers, due to appear here August 27th. It is an epidemic because they are coming here to induce others to join their ranks and it is unfortunate that some of the weaker minded are susceptible to their fallacious teachings unless something is done by the loyal Americans of this area.

By 7 o'clock on the evening of August 27, hundreds of anti-Robeson demonstrators on foot and in cars were led by members of the American Legion to the concert grounds. They blocked the entrance with a truck and huge rocks. People arriving for the concert had to slow down. Many were pulled from their cars and beaten.

It was only a matter of time before a fight broke out between demonstrators and 42 male concertgoers stationed at the entrance. The line of 42 held, all the while singing "We shall not—we shall not be moved!" even though they were being pelted with bottles and rocks. The cars and buses filled with would-be concertgoers had to turn back.

By 7:30, Paul Robeson had arrived at the train station in Peekskill. Those meeting him explained what was happening and drove partway to the concert grounds. Up ahead, gangs were inspecting the passengers in each car. The driver of Robeson's car turned around and drove out of danger to the house of a friendly supporter.

Although there were local police stationed near the entrance of the Lakelands Acres picnic grounds, they did not try to prevent the riot. As the number of demonstrators grew, the group of 42 retreated to protect the women and children back near the concert stage. The mob built a bonfire with concert chairs and continued to fight the vastly outnumbered concertgoers.

At 10 o'clock, the New York State Police finally arrived. They took a dozen concertgoers to the hospital. Fortunately, no one had been killed. Amazingly, no one was arrested.

The next day, August 28, a group of 350 citizens met near

The Peekskill riots. Anti-Robeson protesters attacked concertgoers at the August 27 and September 4, 1949, concerts.

Peekskill and discussed inviting Robeson back. They did not want to be intimidated. Yet, the commander of the local American Legion post had boasted: "Our objective was to prevent the Paul Robeson concert and I think our objective was reached."

The *New York Times* of August 29 echoed the sentiment of the newly formed Westchester Committee for Law and Order, which supported Robeson: "Mr. Robeson, whatever his other qualities, is one of this generation's most magnificent singers. . . . We defend his right to carry his art to whatever peaceably assembled groups of people he wishes."

On August 30, approximately 3,000 people joined a rally at the Golden Gate Ballroom in Harlem. Many people spoke, but the crowd was waiting to hear Paul Robeson.

"We are a part of a very historic departure," Robeson told the crowd. "This means that from now on we take the offensive. *We* take it! We'll have our meetings and concerts all over these

United States. . . . I'll be back with my friends in Peekskill."

Two days later a second concert was scheduled to be held on September 4 at 2 o'clock. The location would be what had once been the Hollow Brook Country Club. Only a mile from the first concert site, it was now land grown to high grass.

This time more than 2,500 volunteers, many of them union workers from New York City, arrived to protect the concertgoers. By midday, these volunteers ringed the 20,000 concertgoers to protect them from the 8,000 anti-Robeson demonstrators. The anti-Robeson slogan for the demonstration, plastered on signs and bumper stickers, was "Wake Up America!—Peekskill Did!"

In addition to the local police, there were also 300 state police

Demonstrators hanged a dummy of Paul Robeson outside the town of Peekskill to show their opposition to his beliefs.

on hand. Many of them stood by smiling or joking with the anti-Robeson demonstrators.

At 2 o'clock in the afternoon the concert began. The first to sing was folksinger Pete Seeger. One of his songs was one he had recently written, "If I Had a Hammer." After a few others sang, and pianists Ray Lev and Leonid Hambro played classical music, it was time for Paul Robeson.

A group of 15 men encircled Robeson to protect him from sniper fire. (Two snipers were later found hiding in the woods.) Robeson did not speak. He cupped his hand against his ear, his customary gesture helping him to hear his voice, and he began to sing. He let his voice speak for him. His first song was "Let my People Go":

> When Israel was in Egyptland,
> Let my people go!

Guarded and protected by friends, Robeson sings folk songs, spirituals, and other songs at the 1949 Peekskill concert.

Oppressed so hard, they could not stand,
Let my people go!
Go down, Moses,
Way down in Egyptland.
Tell old Pharaoh
To let my people go.

For the last song of his concert Robeson sang his signature song, "Ol' Man River." And as he had done when he sang before the troops in Spain, he changed the words to "I must keep fightin' until I'm dyin'."

The concert over, Robeson was taken from the scene by car. Blankets had been placed over the windows, and Robeson lay flat on the floor. Robeson escaped without incident. Many of the concertgoers, however, were not as fortunate.

Pete Seeger described what happened next:

After the great concert was over, the audience of thousands got into cars to drive home. The police . . . stood at the gate, ordering all cars to turn right. Along that road were stationed men with waist-high piles of stones which they heaved at every car. Ten thousand car windows must have been smashed that day.

A CBS radio reporter reported this from the scene as violence once again erupted:

Hundreds and hundreds of people here. If there's a serious outbreak, it will be very bad. The situation has gotten very tense here. There is no longer any order to the parade—just men moving back and forth on the highway, blocking the entrance to the concert area. Skirmishes are breaking out all over here. —The police—are beating up a Negro. They're clubbing him. —He's right here. . . .

One of those beaten by state troopers and deputy sheriffs was Eugene Ballard, the first African American aviator to serve in

World War I. This was not a vague eyewitness report. A series of photographs shows the beating in graphic detail.

Scores of other less prominent Americans were also beaten by the mob. More than 150 of them had been injured. It wasn't until the early morning that the last of the concertgoers had escaped.

One of the first courageous people to speak out against the Peekskill riots was Eleanor Roosevelt, the wife of former President Franklin D. Roosevelt. "I dislike everything Paul Robeson is now saying," she said. "I still believe, however, that if he wants to give a concert or speak his mind in public no one should prevent him from doing so."

The governor of New York State, Thomas E. Dewey, ordered an investigation. This investigation, far from impartial, issued a final report that found no fault with the demonstrators nor with the local police and state troopers.

Robeson continued to give concerts—Cleveland, Detroit, Washington, D.C.—although it was becoming more and more difficult to do so. In Los Angeles, the city council tried to cancel the concert. Advertisements in local newspapers warned people to stay away. Even so, 15,000 people showed up to hear Robeson.

"I shall take my voice," declared Robeson, "wherever there are those who want to hear the melody of freedom or the words that might inspire hope and courage in the face of despair and fear."

Overseas, Robeson remained as popular as ever. In May, he traveled to London for a World Peace Council rally, singing songs in Chinese, Russian, and English for a crowd of 20,000.

Internationally, the cold war was heating up. In 1949, Communists gained control of China, and the Soviet Union tested its first atomic bomb. Tensions increased between the Communist dictatorship of North Korea and the U.S.–supported government in South Korea. Then on June 25, 1950, the North Koreans equipped with Soviet-made weapons invaded South Korea. This action was immediately condemned by the United Nations. On June 27, President Harry S. Truman sent American ships and airplanes to Korea. And in a week's time U.N. troops, most of whom were Americans, were on their way to assist the South Koreans. The ensuing three-year Korean War heightened anti-Communist feelings in the United States.

Robeson spoke out against this military involvement of the United States. "They will know that if we don't stop our armed adventure in Korea today," he said, "tomorrow it will be Africa. . . . I have said it before and say it again, that the place for the Negro people to fight for their freedom is here at home. . . ."

One month later, the U.S. State Department canceled Paul Robeson's passport. "This action is taken because the Department considers that Paul Robeson's travel abroad would be contrary to the best interests of the United States." Soon afterward the passports of Essie Robeson and Paul Robeson Jr. were also revoked.

Few voices were raised in protest. It seemed that most Americans went along with the opinion expressed in an editorial in the *New York Herald Tribune:* "The State Department acts correctly in cancelling Paul Robeson's passport. . . . Mr. Robeson's record as an agitator . . . is well known. . . . This is not the sort of unofficial ambassador we want roaming the world under American passport."

One who did express outrage was W. E. B. Du Bois, the African American educator, editor, and writer. Du Bois and his wife, Shirley Graham, had also had their passports canceled. Calling Robeson "the best known American on earth to the largest number of human beings," Du Bois said, "Only in his native land is he without honor and rights."

When the Council on African Affairs tried to rent Madison Square Garden for a rally to protest Robeson's loss of a passport, they were turned down. Madison Square Garden refused because this group was on the U.S. attorney general's list of subversive organizations. (Organizations on the list had no opportunity to challenge their being listed. Once listed, they often lost their tax-exempt status and could easily be denied the use of meeting places.) So instead, Paul Robeson and 300 supporters met on September 9 on a street corner in Harlem to protest. Robeson told the crowd that he had been "politely imprisoned."

The U.S. State Department's policy of denying passports to certain individuals was soon reinforced by a new law. One of the provisions of the McCarran Act (also known as the Internal

Security Act of 1950) passed by Congress was that Communists would be denied passports. Although President Truman vetoed this bill on September 22, the Congress overrode his veto on the following day.

One way that Robeson was still able to be heard was by writing the column "Here's My Story" in the monthly journal called *Freedom* that he assisted in establishing in November 1950. In his first column Robeson once again explained what he was fighting for: "I fight for the right of the Negro people and other oppressed labor-driven Americans to have decent homes, decent jobs, and the dignity that belongs to every human being! . . . This little paper is begun to help make that determination a reality, and I am proud to be connected with it."

In December 1950, Robeson filed suit against Secretary of State Dean Acheson and the U.S. State Department. His lawyers argued before the District Court that his passport should be returned to him because having canceled it not only had violated his rights under the First Amendment of the U.S. Constitution, but it had also inhibited his ability to make a living. But in April 1951, Robeson's case was dismissed. That year there was some good news, however, as the Robesons became grandparents.

In January 1952, Robeson was invited to sing in Canada in the city of Vancouver, British Columbia. Traveling to Canada did not require a passport. Nevertheless, the State Department invoked a law first passed during World War I that allowed it to prevent the travel of certain citizens "during the existence of the national emergency." If Robeson crossed over to Canada, he would be subject to a $10,000 fine and five years in prison. Robeson remained in Seattle and sang to the members of the United Mine, Mill and Smelter Workers Union via a telephone attached to a loudspeaker at the convention in Vancouver.

Here was a person who had once sung in the world's leading concert halls reduced to singing over the telephone. A bass-baritone who had once commanded $2,000 a concert, now working for $300 or even for nothing. A free spirit who was once welcomed the world over, now restricted by what Robeson described as "a sort of domestic house arrest and confinement." In the words of Andrew Young, later a mayor of Atlanta and the U.S.

representative to the U.N., Robeson was being "buried alive politically." Or as Eric Bentley, a teacher and critic, observed, the U.S. government was making Robeson into an "unperson."

In May, Robeson was once again not allowed to cross into Canada. Instead, he was able to sing to a combined Vancouver and American crowd of 40,000 at Peace Arch Park by remaining on the U.S. side of the border.

Paul Robeson's commitment to his beliefs was certainly exacting a high price. Concert halls would not allow his concerts. Radio stations would not play his songs. His records were removed from record stores. Although Robeson had made more than 300 records during his career, it was virtually impossible to find any of them in record stores. Even his athletic honors of being named to the All-American first team in 1917 and 1918 were taken away. (To this day, those two years remain the only ones with All-American teams that are listed as having only 10 men instead of 11.)

"I have been deprived of my livelihood," Robeson told Walter White in an article for *Ebony* magazine. "I have been stopped from functioning as an artist, which means that I have been denied the right to be a full human being. . . . Even if they had put me on trial and found me guilty of something there would have been a limit to my term of imprisonment. I'd be free now."

Paul Robeson was even prevented from appearing on television. Here is how it happened. Eleanor Roosevelt had contacted him to appear on her TV show, *Today with Mrs. Roosevelt*. However, as soon as executives at NBC heard that the show would be dealing with "The Negro in American Political Life" and would feature Paul Robeson, it was canceled. "We are doubtful that Robeson will ever appear on NBC except under circumstances beyond our control," said a network vice-president. It was the first time anyone had ever been forbidden to appear on American television.

CHAPTER NINE

The Song Is Silenced

In December 1952, Paul Robeson was awarded one of the 1952 International Stalin Peace Prizes given by the Soviet Union. Although this 100,000-ruble prize (approximately $25,000) may have helped financially, it did not enhance his case for regaining a passport.

The U.S. government tried to collect taxes on this prize. Usually, gifts and prizes such as this one are not taxed. However, the government claimed that the prize was for services rendered. In 1958, Robeson finally won his case against the Internal Revenue Service and did not owe any taxes on this prize.

The Stalin Peace Prize also represented a temporary setback in official U.S. government policy from 1951 to 1957 to pressure foreign governments "from honoring Robeson as a great humanitarian and activist for human rights." But in general the U.S. government and the FBI were successful in methodically chipping away at Robeson's stature. As Iago says in Shakespeare's *Othello*:

> But he that filches from me my good name
> Robs me of that which not enriches him
> And makes me poor indeed.

Understandably, money was becoming more of a problem. His income, which had been over $100,000 a year in the 1940s, had been reduced to a few thousand dollars a year in the 1950s. The house in Enfield, Connecticut, had to be sold. Fortunately for the Robesons, however, their money had been wisely invested. So even though Paul Robeson was unable to work, they were still able to live in relative comfort.

One major stumbling block to regaining his passport was Paul Robeson's unwillingness to sign an affidavit declaring that he was not a member of the Communist Party. Robeson maintained that his politics had nothing to do with whether or not he should receive a passport. "Under no conditions would I think of signing any such affidavit . . . ," he said, "it is a complete contradiction of the rights of American citizens."

It is interesting to speculate whether or not Paul Robeson was actually a member of the Communist Party. He loved the Russian people. He felt that the Soviet Union was working to better the conditions of people of color and that this was evident in life there. From his very first visit, he had felt at home. He admittedly didn't know a lot about the prison camps and the killing of millions of people that had gone on, preferring to regard those things as the Soviet Union's internal problems.

Paul Robeson associated with known Communists, whether it was meeting Joseph Stalin or Nikita Khrushchev or getting together with members of the United States Communist Party. He supported those American members when they were on trial or in jail, lending his voice and his prestige to help. Robeson professed the belief that the Communists were engaged in a struggle to make a better life for everyone.

But was he actually a member of the Communist Party? The director of the FBI, J. Edgar Hoover, had spent years unsuccessfully trying to find evidence that he was. The fact was that in 1951 Robeson had volunteered to join. However, his offer had been turned down because it was felt that his standing in the black community would be lowered. And if that were to happen, his effectiveness to the Communist Party would also be decreased.

If anything, Robeson believed in "scientific socialism," a term used to refer to the Communist doctrine know today as Marxism. As he later wrote: "On many occasions I have expressed my belief in the principles of scientific socialism, my deep conviction that for all mankind a socialist society represents an advance to a higher stage of life. . . ."

Nevertheless, the years of constant surveillance by the FBI were beginning to take their toll. To have agents always following him, to have his mail opened, to have his telephone calls tapped—these invasions of privacy had started to have a profound negative impact on his psychological stability.

One aspect of paranoia is the tendency of an individual to be excessively distrustful and suspicious of others. If a person were to find himself or herself in the position that Paul Robeson found himself, to be paranoid would not be an abnormal reaction.

It was also demoralizing for a singer not to be able to sing. Because he could no longer travel, the world's concert halls were no longer available to Robeson. His only available audience in the United States was usually small and radical, politically associated with views and policies of extreme change. It was equally difficult for an actor not to be able to act. Plays and movies were no longer being offered to him.

When a person loses something, he or she is often depressed. In psychology this is known as a reactive depression. It is a normal reaction. What is needed is support. Verbal support at times; quiet support at others.

Robeson began experiencing health problems. He underwent prostate surgery. He had bouts of depression. His mood swings went from manic activity when he worked tirelessly on a book about pentatonic scale theory to debilitating depression when he closed the curtains and never left his room. Also with his lack of exercise and poor eating habits, his weight ballooned to 278 pounds. "He is a very *stubborn* person when it comes to not looking out for himself. . . ," said, a community organizer living in California where she worked to improve her neighborhood.

After the sale of the Robeson estate in Connecticut, Essie Robeson lived in a hotel in Manhattan, while Paul Robeson stayed with friends in the city. Their second grandchild was born in 1953. Although they were not living together, the Robesons became closer in their politics.

On July 7, 1953, Eslanda "Essie" Robeson even appeared before Joseph McCarthy's Senate Investigating Committee. She was questioned by the committee about whether they had a right to know if she were a member of a party committed to the overthrow of the U.S. government.

"I don't know anybody that is dedicated to overthrowing the government by force and violence," Essie Robeson replied. "The only force and violence I know is what I have experienced and seen in this country, and it has not been by Communists."

In 1954, Paul Robeson moved in with his brother the

Reverend Benjamin Robeson, who was pastor of the Mother A.M.E. Zion Church in Harlem. As Paul Robeson was later to write about the influence of his brother:

> My brother's love which enfolds me is a precious, living bond with the man, now forty years dead, who more than anyone else influenced my life—my father, Reverend William Drew Robeson. It is not just that Ben is my older brother, but he reminds me so much of Pop that his house seems to glow with the pervading spirit of that other Reverend Robeson, my wonderful, beloved father.

In July 1955, Robeson again filed suit to have his passport reinstated. The State Department maintained that he would have to sign an affidavit as to whether or not he was a member of the Communist Party. Robeson again refused. He claimed that he was "not allowed to travel because of my friendship—open, spoken friendship—for the Soviet people and the peoples of all the world." The government claimed that he could not get back his passport because he did not sign the affidavit.

After living a year with Ben in his parsonage, Paul in the winter of 1955 moved back in with Essie, who was now living in a house at 16 Jumel Terrace in Harlem. Paul was in need of her steadying influence and her practical approach to things. Essie preferred to struggle with the problems of their difficult marriage rather than to live outside of it.

In May 1956, Robeson had fallen into a deep depression. In July, he had to appear before the House Un-American Activities Committee (HUAC). As he had so often done before, he rallied to overcome a difficulty.

Paul Robeson's appearance before the chairman, the four committee members, and two staff members of the HUAC on July 13 was forceful and impressive. When Richard Arens, the director of the staff, and Gordon H. Scherer, a committee member and congressperson from Ohio, asked if he were a member of the Communist Party, Robeson replied: "What do you mean by the Communist Party? As far as I know it is a legal party

Despite Robeson's controversial political views, enthusiastic
crowds such as this one in Harlem in 1955 still greeted him.

like the Republican Party and the Democratic Party."

Arens asked if Robeson had been known as John Thomas in
the Communist Party. Robeson leaned forward and looked his
questioner right in the eye. "My name is Paul Robeson, and anything I have to say or stand for I have said in public all over the
world, and that is why I am here today."

"Why do you not stay in Russia?" asked Scherer.

"Because my father was a slave," answered Robeson, "and my
people died to build this country, and I am going to stay here and
have a part of it just like you."

When Arens asked if Robeson had changed his mind about
Stalin, Robeson answered, "Whatever has happened to Stalin,
gentlemen, is a question for the Soviet Union. . . ."

At another point, Robeson objected to the idea set forth by
Chairman Francis E. Walter that Robeson did not appreciate all
he had. "I challenge very deeply, and very sincerely, the fact that
the success of a few Negroes, including myself or Jackie Robinson
can make up . . . for thousands of Negro families in the South. My
father was a slave, and I have cousins who are sharecroppers and

I do not see my success in terms of myself. That is the reason, my own success has not meant what it should mean. I have sacrificed literally hundreds of thousands, if not millions, of dollars for what I believe in."

At other times in answer to other questions, Robeson invoked the Fifth Amendment. Part of the original Bill of Rights, this amendment has roots that go back to the 1200s. Its purpose is to protect witnesses from having to testify against themselves. There was also another explanation for why Robeson refused to answer certain questions. Although Robeson may not have been a Communist, many of his friends were. If he had answered the question about himself, he would have been asked to implicate his friends.

One of the reasons that Paul Robeson caused such trouble for the members of Congress on these committees was that he had been trained in the law. Thus, he could not be intimidated. He knew that it was perfectly legal to point out that the Fifth Amendment protected Americans' right not to be forced to testify against themselves. Therefore, he was not committing a crime by claiming the protection of the Fifth Amendment. "[T]he Fifth Amendment has nothing to do with criminality," said Robeson at one point. "The Chief Justice of the Supreme Court, [Earl] Warren, has been very clear on that in many speeches that the Fifth Amendment does not have anything to do with the inference of criminality."

Paul Robeson testifies before the House Un-American Activities Committee in 1956.

Paul Robeson was nothing if not clear and forthright. On July 14, 1956, he read a statement to the press that he had not been able to read the day before to the committee. Part of this statement concerned his earlier appearance before the Tenney Committee on Un-American Activities in California: "In 1946, at a hearing in California, I testified under oath that I was not a member of the Communist Party. Since then I have refused to give testimony to that fact. There is no mystery in this. I have made it a matter of principle to refuse to comply with any demand that infringes upon the Constitutional rights of all Americans."

No matter what anyone thought about Paul Robeson, it could not be denied that here was a person who had the courage of his convictions. And he had sacrificed dearly for them.

In the summer of 1957, the State Department eased its travel restrictions for Robeson. He would now be able to travel to destinations where a U.S. passport was not required (Alaska, American Samoa, Guam, Hawaii, Puerto Rico, and the Virgin Islands). It was a break in the case that had become an international embarrassment for the United States.

The next year, 1958, Paul Robeson came out with *Here I Stand,* a book that was in part the story of his early life and in part about the political issues that had defined his life and thought. Written with the assistance of Lloyd L. Brown, this book spelled out what Robeson felt was important.

First of all, it set out his sense of identification with all African Americans:

> I am a Negro. The house I live in is in Harlem— this city within a city, Negro metropolis of America. And now as I write of things that are urgent in my mind and heart, I feel the press of all that is around me here where I live, at home among my people.

Second, it contained his feelings for his country:

> I am an American. From my window I gaze out upon a scene that reminds me how deep-going are the roots of my people in this land. Across the street,

carefully preserved as an historic shrine, is a colonial mansion that served as a headquarters for General George Washington in 1776. . . . [A]mong those who came to offer help in that desperate hour was my great-great-grandfather [on his mother's side]. He was Cyrus Bustill, who was born a slave in New Jersey and had managed to purchase his freedom. He became a baker and it is recorded that George Washington thanked him for supplying bread to the starving Revolutionary Army.

Another important point in *Here I Stand* was the dispelling of the notion that Robeson had ever been a member of the Communist Party. Although he refused to sign an affidavit that he was not a member, Robeson made it quite clear in his book:

My views concerning the Soviet Union and my warm feelings of friendship for the peoples of that land, and the friendly sentiments which they have often expressed toward me, have been pictured as something quite sinister by Washington officials and other spokesmen for the dominant white group in our country. It has been alleged that I am part of some kind of "international conspiracy."

The truth is: *I am not and never have been involved in any international conspiracy or any other kind, and do not know anyone who is.*

Robeson also detailed his life as an activist and his struggle for human rights:

Yes, I have been active for African freedom for many years and I will never cease that activity no matter what the State Department or anybody else thinks about it. This is my right—as a Negro, as an American, as a man!

Although this was a book by one of the best-known people in

the world, there was practically no mention of it in the mainstream press in the United States. The only reviews appeared in African American newspapers and overseas in foreign newspapers. In spite of this lack of publicity, the book sold 25,000 copies in the first six months.

Soon after the publication of *Here I Stand*, Robeson came out with his first recording for a major record company since his travel had been restricted.

On April 9, 1958, Robeson's 60th birthday was celebrated by people in 27 different countries. In India, Prime Minister Jawaharlal Nehru hailed Robeson as "one of the greatest artists of our generation." Nehru went on to say that Robeson had "represented and suffered for a cause which should be dear to all of us—the cause of human dignity."

A month later Robeson appeared at a sold-out concert at New York City's Carnegie Hall. At 60, his voice might not have been what it once was. It now seemed strained and pinched rather than full and clear like a bell. However, as he sang his way through Bach's "Christ Lag in Todesbanden," the "Chinese Children's Song," "Didn't My Lord Deliver Daniel," "Every Time I Feel the Spirit," to his last song, "We Are Climbing Jacob's Ladder," his voice grew in power and clarity. And there were no doubts that Paul Robeson still retained his commanding presence and magnetism.

In June 1958, the Supreme Court ruled on two important cases. The Court found that a person's political beliefs were not grounds for the secretary of state to refuse a passport. In addition, the Court stated that the Passport Division of the State Department could not require someone to sign an affidavit pertaining to whether or not he or she was a member of the Communist Party.

These rulings had a direct bearing on Robeson's case, and in two weeks' time Robeson was issued a passport. Once again, the Robesons were free to travel.

CHAPTER TEN

The End of the Road

On July 10, 1958, Essie and Paul Robeson boarded a BOAC flight for the trip to London. Two weeks after their arrival, Paul Robeson had a special half-hour concert on British television. "[H]e is one of those," commented the reviewer for the London *Times*, "whom age shows no signs of withering." Robeson also signed a contract to play the title role in *Othello* for the 100th season celebration of theater at Stratford-upon-Avon.

In August, the Robesons were off to Moscow where Robeson sang a concert before 18,000 people at the Lenin Sports Stadium. The crowd clapped and clapped after listening to the folksongs he sang in various languages.

After returning to England, Robeson sang in October in a landmark cathedral before 4,000 people. " I remember that Sunday evening," wrote Shirley Graham Du Bois, "when he sang in London's famous St. Paul's Cathedral—his magnificent voice rising to the vaulted dome, reflected in the stained glass windows and resting upon the hushed crowd like a benediction."

Later that fall, Paul Robeson and Larry Brown were off on a 60-city concert tour of Great Britain.

By New Year's Eve, the Robesons were back in Moscow. For the grand finale of the Kremlin Ball with Premier Nikita S. Khrushchev and other Soviet dignitaries in attendance, Robeson went on stage to sing with the other entertainers. Not long afterward, the Robesons were admitted to the Kremlin Hospital: Paul for bronchitis and exhaustion; Essie for cancer of the uterus.

After a two-month period of recuperation, Paul Robeson left his wife in Russia to return to England and begin rehearsals for *Othello*. With Tony Richardson directing, Sam Wanamaker as Iago, and Mary Ure as Desdemona, the play opened on April 7, 1959. Essie Robeson was in the audience on opening night. The reviews were favorable enough to sell out the entire seven-month run. Fortunately for Robeson, he was not under contract to appear in every performance. In fact, by the end of the engagement he was only on stage twice a week.

The following year, Robeson was offered a concert tour he could not refuse: 20 concerts in Australia and New Zealand for the handsome sum of $100,000. While touring "Down Under," Paul Robeson became indignant at the plight of the Aborigines. These original Australians, numbering about 75,000, had been pushed off their land and into the inhospitable desert. He spoke out about their plight.

Back in London, Paul and Essie sorted through the many

A 1959 concert in Vienna, Austria. Robeson continued to speak out against racial segregation and American foreign policy.

offers to put together a schedule for the rest of the year. However, Paul was unable to shake his deep depression. "Terribly lonely," he wrote to his good friend Helen Rosen, "but just doing the best I can. Have altogether failed to find friends over here. Guess I'm to blame. . . ."

Alarmed by his despair, Helen Rosen flew from New York to London. Robeson welcomed her and listened as she attempted to convince him to return to the United States to be with family and friends. But a trip to Moscow had already been planned, and he went through with it.

Robeson soon settled into a whirlwind of activity. Plans were made for concerts, interviews, and a film version of *Othello*. On the night of March 27, 1961, there was a party in Robeson's hotel room. In the early morning hours, Paul Robeson went into the bathroom, took out a razor, and cut his wrists. Doctors said that Robeson's suicide attempt had been brought on by a "depressive paranoiac psychosis." Paul Robeson Jr., however, became very suspicious about the circumstances. Fearing that the United States Central Intelligence Agency might somehow be involved, the son flew to Moscow to be with his father.

When not at his bedside, Paul Jr. attempted to solve the mystery of what had happened that night. Incredibly, less than two weeks following his arrival, Paul Jr. also attempted to commit suicide. He had tried to jump out the window of his hotel room.

Both father and son were in the hospital together and then later recovering in a sanatorium. In June, the father flew back to London and the son returned to the United States. But Paul Robeson soon had a relapse, and his wife had him returned to the hospital in Moscow. By September, he was once again in London. This time his good mental health lasted only two days. It was then that Essie Robeson discovered her husband in the apartment, lying on his side, curled up, with his arms and legs drawn up near his chest.

Robeson was taken to the Priory, a private psychiatric hospital in Roehampton. His doctors there found him "in a depressed, agitated state with many ideas of persecution." Dr. Brian Acker prescribed electroconvulsive therapy, also known as ECT or shock therapy.

The use of ECT was not so unusual at that time to treat severe depression. However, it was started before treatment with drugs was tried. Also, there was no talk therapy. Robeson was not placed in a situation where he was able to express himself one-on-one with a psychologist or psychiatrist. In addition, the number of shocks may have been excessive. By the following April, Robeson had received 24 shock treatments. At first Essie Robeson did not tell their son about the decision to use ECT. When Paul Jr. found out, he was furious. He believed that shock treatment might ruin his father's memory or even destroy part of his brain.

For the next several months Robeson went back and forth between their London apartment and the psychiatric hospital. During a period when he was feeling relatively well, Paul and Essie Robeson went to the U.S. Embassy to renew their passports. Everything seemed to be in order. However, some weeks later the Robesons were told they had to sign affidavits about whether they were currently or had in the past year been members of the Communist Party. Essie promptly signed hers. Paul refused until two trusted friends, John Abt and Ben Davis Jr., convinced him that this was an old battle that had already been won.

By 1963, Robeson had received 54 electric shocks, was on a heavy dose of medication, but was still suffering bouts of depression. On the advice of a friend, the Robesons flew to the Buch Clinic in East Berlin. The doctors at the Buch Clinic took Robeson off his heavy dosage of drugs. He had his ups and downs, but he seemed to be getting better on a lighter dosage.

Essie Robeson, on the other hand, received some rough news from the doctors when they examined her. She had terminal cancer. Instead of giving in to the sickness, she decided to live life to the fullest. Just as she had not told her husband for several months about his brother Ben's death from cancer the previous summer, she also decided to keep the state of her health a secret from him.

In December 1963, Paul Robeson made a decision of his own. He wanted to return to the United States. He may have become passive and noncommittal about many things, but this was something he was sure about. On December 22, 1963, the Robesons returned home. They were greeted at the airport by

Paul Jr. and Marilyn Robeson and their two children, Susan and David, plus a flock of reporters.

Back at the house at 16 Jumel Terrace in Harlem, the Robesons settled into their new life. Essie was determined to get as much done as possible in the time she had remaining. Paul, on the other hand, sometimes had his good days and sometimes had his bad days.

Essie and Paul Jr. did their best to keep Paul away from the press. They wanted to protect his privacy, not allowing others to see him when he was experiencing difficulties. But Paul Robeson finally did make a statement to the press on August 28, 1964. That was the first anniversary of the 1963 March on Washington, which had been the largest civil rights demonstration in American history. Within a year of that march, Congress had passed the Civil Rights Act of 1964, which outlawed discrimination in hotels, restaurants, and other public accommodations. Paul Robeson's statement to the press said in part:

Paul Robeson is greeted by his son, Paul Robeson Jr., after finally returning to the United States in late 1963.

When I wrote in my book, *Here I Stand* in 1958, that "the time is now," some people thought that perhaps my watch was fast (and maybe it was a little), but most of us seem to be running on the same time now.

The "power of Negro action," of which I then wrote, has changed from an idea to a reality that is manifesting itself throughout our land. The concept of mass militancy, or mass action, is no longer deemed "too radical" in Negro life.

Things went so well in 1965 that Robeson even wrote a short piece about W. E. B. Du Bois. "Casting my mind back," Robeson wrote, "my first clear memory of Dr. Du Bois was my pride in his recognized scholarship and authority in his many fields of work and writing. In high school and at college our teachers often referred us to standard reference works on sociology, race relations, Africa and world affairs. I remember feeling great pride when the books and articles proved to be by our Dr. Du Bois, and often loaned these to my fellow-students. . . ."

In March 1965, *Freedomways* magazine held a party for Robeson to celebrate the publication of his article. Robeson even sang, marking the first time in four years he had sung in public.

Freedomways magazine also sponsored a 67th birthday party for Paul Robeson at the Americana Hotel in New York City in April 1965. At the end of the evening Paul Robeson told the 2,000 people: "It is clear that the Negro people are claiming their rights and they are in every way determined to have those rights and nothing can turn us back! Most important is the recognition that achieving these demands in no way lessens the democratic rights of white American citizens. On the contrary, it will enormously strengthen the base of democracy for all Americans."

Paul Robeson then went on to say how important it was for everyone to find "a living connection, deeper and stronger, between the Negro people and the great mass of white Americans who are indeed our natural allies in the struggle for democracy." At the conclusion of his speech, the audience stood and cheered the legend before them.

Essie Robeson felt so good about how well her husband was getting along that she encouraged a plan to make a goodwill trip to California. There they had a full schedule, sometimes appearing at more than one event on the same day. All went well at first, but then both Robesons became so exhausted that they had to cancel the final week and a half and return home.

Paul Robeson again fell into a deep depression. In June, he cut himself with a pair of scissors. The next day he was taken to Gracie Square, a psychiatric hospital in New York City.

From comments Paul Robeson had made at other times, he hated to let anyone down. He had learned at an early age that you always give everything your best. Later in life, when his abilities and energy began to fail, it was very difficult for him to adjust.

By late summer, Essie Robeson was also in the hospital. Both of them were back home by early fall. But it was only a matter of time for her. Late in November, she was back in the hospital. Early in the morning on December 13, 1965, Eslanda Goode Robeson died. Robeson was not even able to attend the funeral.

With his anchor gone, Paul Robeson was seemingly cut adrift. However, his sister, Marian Robeson Forsythe, who lived in Philadelphia, came to the rescue and took over the helm. With help from Paul Jr., they made sure that he was comfortable and safe. Life passed with a heartrending sameness for this one-time All-American athlete, this world-famous singer, this stage and movie actor, this political activist once trailed by the FBI. As his son remarked of his father's condition: "basically he wasn't there."

The last decade of Paul Robeson's life was a pianissimo after the crescendo, an anticlimax after a life of curtain calls. People would often forget about him. Some would not remember if he were still alive or not. Many young people had never even heard of Paul Robeson.

But from time to time there would be reminders.

The National Educational Network (now PBS) produced an Emmy Award-winning documentary on his life. *Ebony* magazine declared Robeson one of the "ten most important black men in American history." *Here I Stand* was reprinted by Beacon Press, and this time it was reviewed in the mainstream press. Professor

113

Sterling Stuckey wrote in his review in the *New York Times*: "Robeson's fate illustrates the extent to which guardians of the culture are willing, when frightened, to attempt to blot from history a man's meaning, his very existence."

In 1972, Rutgers University opened the Paul Robeson Campus Center. And on April 15, 1973, there was a 75th birthday celebration. This salute to Paul Robeson was held at New York City's famed Carnegie Hall. Pete Seeger and Harry Belafonte sang, the actors James Earl Jones and Sidney Poitier offered tributes, and Dolores Huerta of the United Farm Workers spoke. Although the guest of honor himself could not be there in that great hall that night, his voice was. As a hush fell over the audience in the cavernous auditorium, a tape recorder played the still vibrant voice of Paul Robeson:

> Warmest thanks to all the many friends here and throughout the world who have sent me greetings on my 75th birthday. Though I have not been able to be active for several years, I want you to know that I am the same Paul, dedicated as ever to the worldwide cause of humanity for freedom, peace and brotherhood.
>
> Here at home, my heart is with the continuing struggles of my own people to achieve complete liberation from the racist domination, and to gain for all black Americans and the other minority groups not only equal rights but an equal share. . . .

One final reminder that he was still around was that in 1974 the FBI at last canceled its investigation of Paul Robeson.

On December 28, 1975, Paul Robeson suffered a heart attack and was taken to the Presbyterian Medical Center in Philadelphia. He lingered on until January 23, 1976, when he finally died at the age of 77. The official cause was a stroke, "complications arising from severe cerebral vascular disorder."

The funeral of Paul Leroy Robeson was held four days later in Harlem at the Mother African Methodist Episcopal Zion Church. This was the same church where his brother, Ben Robeson, had been the minister for 27 years. Established in 1895, it was also the same church where Frederick Douglass and Harriet Tubman, two early fighters for freedom for African Americans, had attended services.

One of the speakers was Paul Robeson Jr., who spoke about that "great and gentle warrior," his father:

> And so I come to speak of both the disappointments and the triumphs of Paul Robeson's last years—disappointment because illness forced him into complete retirement; triumph because he retired undefeated and unrepentant. He never regretted the stands he took, because almost forty years ago, in 1937, he made his basic choice. He said then: "The artist must elect to fight for freedom or for slavery. I have made my choice. I had no alternative."

The eulogy of Bishop J. Clinton Hoggard was taken from Paul Robeson's rendition of "Joe Hill": "Don't mourn for me, but live for freedom's cause."

Perhaps it is appropriate for Paul Robeson himself to have the final word. When he played Othello on the stage, he would give voice to words that could also serve as his epitaph:

> I have done the state some service and they know't.
> No more of that. I pray you, in your letters,
> When you shall these unlucky deeds relate,
> Speak of me as I am. Nothing extenuate,
> Nor set down aught in malice. . . .

1898	Paul Leroy Robeson is born on April 9 in Princeton, New Jersey. Paul is the youngest of Maria Louisa Bustill and William Drew Robeson's five children.
1915	Robeson graduates as an honor student from Somerville High School and wins four-year scholarship to Rutgers College.
1918	Robeson earns Phi Beta Kappa honors and becomes a two-time All-American football player. He also excels as a debater, a singer, and an actor.
1919	Robeson graduates from Rutgers College, the valedictorian of his class. He also wins 15 letters in four varsity sports and is elected to Cap and Skull, the senior honor society.
1919	Robeson enters the Columbia University School of Law.
1921	Robeson marries Eslanda Cardozo Goode.
1923	Robeson graduates from Columbia Law School.
1924	Robeson stars in Eugene O'Neill's *The Emperor Jones* and *All God's Chillun Got Wings*. He appears in his first film, *Body and Soul*.
1925	Robeson and Lawrence Brown give first concert together.
1927	Paul Robeson Jr. is born.
1928	Robeson sings role of Joe the Riverman in Jerome Kern's *Show Boat* in London.
1929	Robeson sings at Carnegie Hall in New York City.
1930	Robeson stars in the London production of *Othello*.

1933	Robeson stars in the film version of O'Neill's *The Emperor Jones.*
1934	Robeson stars in *Sanders of the River* and visits Soviet Union for the first time.
1935	Robeson appears in the film of *Show Boat* and in the play *Stevedore.*
1936	Robeson stars in film *Song of Freedom.*
1937	Robeson stars in three films: *Jericho, Big Fella,* and *King Solomon's Mines.*
1938	The Spanish Civil War is halted for a day as Robeson sings for the troops on the front line. Robeson is featured in play *Plant in the Sun.*
1939	Robeson sings "Ballad for Americans" and makes film *The Proud Valley.*
1940-1943	Robeson sings in concert halls and at many political rallies.
1942	Robeson performs in the film *Tales of Manhattan* and narrates in the documentary *Native Land.*
1943	Robeson stars in *Othello* on Broadway in New York City. The play sets record for Shakespeare on Broadway with 296 performances.
1944	Robeson receives Donaldson Award for Outstanding Lead Performance and the Academy of Arts and Letters gold medal for diction, both for *Othello.*
1949	Robeson speaks to the World Peace Congress in Paris.
1949	Robeson sings at a Peekskill, New York, concert, disrupted by violent demonstrators.
1950	Robeson's passport is taken away by U.S. State Department.

1952	Robeson receives the International Stalin Peace Prize.
1958	Robeson's passport is restored, and his book *Here I Stand* is published.
1959	Robeson appears in *Othello* at 100th year anniversary of Shakespearean theater at Stratford-upon-Avon, England.
1960	Robeson travels to Australia and New Zealand for last concert tour.
1965	Eslanda Cardozo Goode Robeson, Paul Robeson's wife, dies.
1972	Paul Robeson Campus Center dedicated at Rutgers University.
1973	Seventy-fifth birthday celebration for Paul Robeson at Carnegie Hall.
1976	Paul Robeson dies on January 23 in Philadelphia, Pennsylvania.

affidavit A sworn written or printed statement of facts, taken voluntarily and under oath before a magistrate or officer.

anarchist A person who believes in, advocates, or promotes the political theory that all governments are unnecessary and undesirable and that society should be based on voluntary cooperation of individuals and groups. Some anarchists advocate the overthrow of organized government by force.

capitalism An economic system in which the means of production are owned by individuals or corporations and the investments are determined by private not governmental decisions. Under capitalism, people own and control private property, and the prices, production, and distribution of goods and services are determined by competition in a free market.

cold war The post–World War II conflict between the United States and its democratic and capitalist allies on one side and the politically unfree Soviet Union and its Communist allies on the other. It did not involve direct military action between the United States and the Soviet Union, but it did include economic, political and military rivalry and mistrust.

collective An agricultural organization in which the work and the profits are shared by its members. In most Communist countries, collectives rented the land from the state and had to provide to the state a set amount of their crops.

communism A system of political and economic beliefs based on the ideas of Marx and Lenin. In theory, private property is eliminated, people own and control the means of production in common, economic goods and services are distributed fairly, and the state plays a minimum role in people's lives. In reality, in the Soviet Union and elsewhere, a dictatorial Communist Party controlled the government and the economy.

crescendo A gradual increase in the volume of a musical piece.

curtain call A performer's appearance requested by audience applause after the end of a play or other performance.

deportation The removal or sending back of an alien (a foreign-born or other person who has not qualified as a citizen) to the country from which he or she came because that person's presence is considered unlawful or inconsistent with the public welfare.

documentary A factual presentation of events, usually in a film or TV program.

fascism A system of political and economic beliefs that places the importance of the nation and often a particular race above the individual. Under fascism, political and economic power are under the tight control of a centralized undemocratic government headed by a dictator who also heads the only political party allowed. Fascism includes the belief that it is right to brutally suppress all opposition to the dictator's policies, which are supposedly designed to favor the good of the nation and the favored race.

folk songs Traditional or composed songs that are in the form of stanzas with refrains and simple melodies. Folk songs are often learned through hearing rather than reading, are often spread through families and close social groups, and are often about routine activities of daily life. Sometimes the topics of folk songs deal with a group's or a country's history. They are usually sung unaccompanied or with simple accompaniment such as a guitar or a dulcimer.

imperialism The policy, practice, and advocacy of extending the power of a nation into other parts of the world in order to gain direct control by occupation or indirect control by political and economic influence. The goals are often to obtain inexpensive sources of raw materials and workers or new markets for the nation's goods and services or new places for investments. The direct beneficiaries of imperialism are supposedly citizens of the imperial nation but often are large corporations and financial institutions.

Iron Curtain The political and military barrier that cut off and isolated the Soviet Union and other Communist-controlled countries from the ideas of—and the communication with and travel to—the rest of the world, particularly democratic and capitalist countries.

left-wing Having to do with the political, social, and economic ideas or policies of people who desire reform or change in established governments and politics in order to achieve greater freedom and well-being for ordinary people. Some leftists are moderates, advocating peaceful reforms that promote greater democracy and democratic socialism. People on the Far Left, however, may advocate extreme measures and communism.

lynching The action of an unofficial, organized band or mob that seizes people charged with or suspected of crimes and illegally punishes them by killing them, all done without legal trial or procedures. Usually the victims are beaten, tortured, mutilated, shot, burned, or hanged until dead.

octave A musical interval composed of eight notes or tones.

pentatonic scale A musical scale in which the tones are arranged like a major scale with the fourth and seventh tones omitted.

pianissimo A musical piece or passage sung or played very softly.

repertoire The list of the plays, operas, songs, musical pieces, or dramatic parts that an actor, singer, or other performer is prepared to perform.

right-wing Having to do with the political, social, and economic ideas or policies of people who oppose change in the established order and favor traditional attitudes and conservative practices. Some rightists are moderates, advocating the peaceful establishment of capitalism and a strong nation-state. People on the Far Right may advocate extreme measures such as authoritarian rule or a Fascist dictatorship.

sit-down strike The stopping of work by employees who remain in their workplace as a protest and as a means to force their employer to give in to demands, usually for higher wages or better working conditions. By remaining in the factory or workshop, striking workers gain publicity and make it difficult for their employer to use replacement workers.

socialism A system of political and economic beliefs in which the means of production are owned and controlled by the state. In theory, private property is limited to personal items, the people own and control the means of production in common, economic goods and services are distributed fairly, and the state makes sure that people's economic and political rights are protected. In practice, socialism has varied greatly. In some countries, a dictatorship holds political power and controls all industry and economic policies, claiming it knows what is best for the people. In other countries, a system of democratic socialism has prevailed: The state owns the larger corporations and financial institutions and attempts to further the people's economic well-being fairly by managing the means of production with decisions made by a democratically elected government.

spirituals Religious songs usually of a deeply emotional character that were developed by African Americans who were enslaved in the southern United States. The musical origins were a blending of white hymns, especially British folk music, and African music, especially traditional music from a variety of West African cultures.

stanzas The division of a poem or lyrics of a song, consisting of a series of lines arranged together in a usually recurring pattern of meter, rhyme, or melody.

stock speculator One who takes great financial risks in buying and selling ownership shares in companies.

BIBLIOGRAPHY

and Recommended Readings

Duberman, Martin Bauml. *Paul Robeson*. New York: Alfred A. Knopf, 1988.

*Ehrlich, Scott. *Paul Robeson: Athlete, Actor, Singer, Activist*. Los Angeles: Melrose Square Publishing, 1989.

Fast, Howard. *Peekskill, USA: A Personal Experience*. New York: Civil Rights Congress, 1951.

Graham, Shirley. *Paul Robeson: Citizen of the World*. New York: Julian Messner, 1946.

*Hamilton, Virginia. *Paul Robeson: The Life and Times of a Free Black Man*. New York: Harper & Row, 1974.

Hoyt, Edwin P. *Paul Robeson: The American Othello*. Cleveland: The World Publishing Company, 1967.

*Larsen, Rebecca. *Paul Robeson: Hero Before His Time*. New York: Franklin Watts, 1989.

O'Neill, Eugene. *The Emperor Jones*. A video recording starring Paul Robeson. Los Angeles: Embassy Home Entertainment, 1987.

Paul Robeson: The Great Forerunner. The Editors of *Freedomways*. New York: Dodd, Mead & Company, 1978.

Robeson, Eslanda Goode. *Paul Robeson, Negro*. New York: Harper & Brothers, 1930.

Robeson, Paul. *Here I Stand*. Boston: Beacon Press, 1972

———. *Paul Robeson, Speaks*. Edited by Philip S. Foner. New York: Citadel Press, 1978.

Robeson, Susan. *The Whole World in His Hands: A Pictorial History of Paul Robeson*. Secaucus, N.J.: Citadel Press, 1981.

*Especially recommended for younger readers.

PLACES TO VISIT

New York, New York

• The Schomburg Center for Research in Black Culture of the New York Public Library.

Philadelphia, Pennsylvania

• Charles L. Blockson Afro-American Collection at Temple University.

• African American State Historical Marker at 4951 Walnut Street where Paul Robeson spent his last years.

Piscataway, New Jersey

• Paul Robeson Cultural Center on the Busch Campus of Rutgers University.

Washington, D.C.

• Paul Robeson Audio-Visual Room of the Moorland-Spingarn Research Library at Howard University Law School.

ACKNOWLEDGMENTS

The author acknowledges with gratitude the use of quotations from the following published works:

Duberman, Martin Bauml, *Paul Robeson*, New York: Alfred A. Knopf, 1988; Ehrlich, Scott, *Paul Robeson: Athlete, Actor, Singer, Activist*, Los Angeles: Melrose Publishing, 1989; Fast, Howard, *Peekskill, USA: A Personal Experience*, New York: Civil Rights Congress, 1951; *Freedomways* editors, *Paul Robeson: The Great Forerunner*, New York: Dodd, Mead, & Company, 1978; Graham, Shirley, *Paul Robeson, Citizen of the World*, New York: Julian Messner; 1946; Hamilton, Virginia, *Paul Robeson: The Life and Times of a Free Black Man*, New York: Harper & Row; Hammerstein II, Oscar, "Ol' Man River" from *Show Boat*; Hoyt, Edwin P., *Paul Robeson: The American Othello*, Cleveland: The World Publishing Company, 1967; Larsen, Rebecca, *Paul Robeson: Hero Before His Time*, New York: Franklin Watts, 1989; LaTouche, John, "Ballad for Americans"; Robeson, Eslanda Goode, *Paul Robeson, Negro*, New York: Harper & Brothers, 1930; Robeson, Paul, *Here I Stand*, Boston: Beacon Press, 1972, and *Paul Robeson Speaks*, edited by Philip S. Foner, New York: Citadel Press, 1978; Robeson, Susan, *The Whole World in His Hands: A Pictorial History of Paul Robeson*, Secaucus, N.J.: Citadel Press, 1981; Sandburg, Carl, "Untitled Poem."

INDEX

Burnham Holmes is a writer and teacher. His most recent titles are *Yogi, Babe, and Magic: The Complete Book of Sports Nicknames* (with Louis Phillips), *Cesar Chavez: Farm Worker Activist* for the American Troublemakers series, *George Eastman* for the Pioneers in Change series, and *The Third Amendment* and *The Fifth Amendment* for The American Heritage History of the Bill of Rights series.

Holmes teaches writing at the School of Visual Arts in New York City. Burnham, Vicki, and their son, Ken, live in New York City and near a lake in Vermont.

James P. Shenton is Professor of History at Columbia University. He has taught American History since 1951. Among his publications are *Robert John Walker, a Politician from Jackson to Lincoln; An Historian's History of the United States*; and *The Melting Pot*. Professor Shenton is a consultant to the National Endowment for the Humanities and has received the Mark Van Doren and Society of Columbia Graduates' Great Teachers Awards. He also serves as a consultant for CBS, NBC, and ABC educational programs.

COVER ILLUSTRATION

Gary McElhaney

MAPS

Go Media, Inc.

PHOTOGRAPHY CREDITS

p.6 Archive Photos; p.12 Somerset County Historical Society; pp. 21, 26 Rutgers University; p.29 Hulton-Deutsch; p.31 Columbia University; p.36 Schomburg Center For Research in Black Culture, New York Public Library; p.47 UPI/Bettmann; p.50 Culver Pictures; p.51 UPI/Bettmann; p.53 The Bettmann Archive; p.56 Schomburg Center For Research in Black Culture, New York Public Library; p.57 UPI/Bettmann; p.58 Culver Pictures; p.60 UPI/Bettmann; p.64 Sovfoto; p.68 © Herbert Gehr, Life Magazine © Time Warner; p.71Schomburg Center For Research in Black Culture, New York Public Library; p.72 The Bettmann Archive; p.79 AP/Wide World; p.81Schomburg Center For Research in Black Culture, New York Public Library; pp.82, 83 UPI/Bettmann; p.85 AP/Wide World; p.86 UPI/Bettmann; p.90 AP/Wide World; p.91 The Bettmann Archive; p.92 AP/Wide World; p.102 courtesy Esther Jackson/Freedomways; p.103 AP/Wide World; pp.108, 111 UPI/Bettmann.